"What a wonderful exploration into the language of intimacy, relationships, and love! In this deeply insightful book, you will be exposed to the key ingredients of an intimate relationship: self-love, self-worth, and self-awareness. I highly recommend this book to anyone interested in engaging in life and love in an empowered way!"

> —**Shefali Tsabary, PhD**, *New York Times* bestselling author and psychologist

"As modern dating increasingly gets reduced to a narrow set of online search algorithms, Alexandra H. Solomon wisely implores readers to turn off the noise, tune into our authentic selves, and cultivate a deeper sense of relational self-awareness. *Loving Bravely* will show you how to go beyond merely swiping left or right, scrolling up and down, and instead live and love in ways that are true to your unique, multidimensional self."

> —**Ian Kerner, PhD, LMFT**, *New York Times* bestselling author of *She Comes First*

"Alexandra H. Solomon has written the best book ever about creating, developing, and nurturing relationships. *Loving Bravely* is very special and unique among books on relationships. First, it is anchored in the scientific knowledge about relationships, yet is engaging and interesting. Second, it speaks to the issues of the twenty-first century for young and mid-life people in relationships. And, it centers primarily on what individuals can do themselves to nurture relationships. This is the manual for any person who wants to nurture and preserve a satisfying relationship."

> —**Jay Lebow, PhD, ABPP**, clinical professor at The Family Institute at Northwestern University, and editor of *Family Process*

"Alexandra H. Solomon has written a clear-eyed, practical guidebook on nothing less than how to love. *Loving Bravely* covers everything from how to shift beyond your own reactivity to how to offer an effective apology. Years of clinical experience shine through a book I'd recommend to anyone interested in loving well."

—**Terry Real**, founder of the Relational Life Institute in
  Massachusetts, and author of *The New Rules of Marriage*

"This is a powerful book that beautifully lays out the path to having a healthier love relationship with others, by first having a healthier love relationship with yourself. Written in an engaging manner and full of practical exercises, this book is a godsend to anyone searching for, but struggling to find, true love in their lives."

—**Kristin Neff, PhD**, associate professor in the department of
  educational psychology at The University of Texas at Austin,
  and author of *Self-Compassion*

"We all want to be in love or fall in love. But as Alexandra H. Solomon so persuasively argues, most of us spend more time learning to drive than learning to love. Clear-eyed and compassionate, Solomon provides step-by-step guidance on how to gain the skills needed to make a relationship—even a good one—deeper, more satisfying, and more intimate. *Loving Bravely* should be required reading for anyone involved in an intimate relationship and compulsory for anyone yearning to have one. As Solomon asks, are you willing to invest in love?"

—**Elsa Walsh**, author of the best-selling *Divided Lives*, and former
  staff writer for *The New Yorker* and *The Washington Post*

"Alexandra H. Solomon's *Loving Bravely* is a terrific guidebook for anyone contemplating or engaged in an intimate relationship. This book brings together Solomon's experience over the last twenty years studying couples, treating couples, immersing herself in couples therapy literature, and lastly, being coupled. First as a graduate student, and then a psychologist and professor at Northwestern University; as a therapist at The Family Institute at Northwestern University; and as a wife, Solomon has lived and breathed close relationships. No one knows this terrain better from both the inside and the outside. The wisdom in this book focuses on the concept of 'know thyself first, fix thyself first, face thyself first.' Loving over the long haul means developing the courage to face yourself and your partner with honesty, integrity, and compassion. *Loving Bravely* provides the keys to becoming a better partner and a better person, not the keys to fixing or changing your partner. I recommend this book to anyone who wants to be a better lover in the truest and deepest sense."

—**Bill Pinsof, PhD, LMFT, ABPP**, founder, chief executive, and
    clinical professor at The Family Institute at Northwestern
    University, 1986-2016; and president of Pinsof Family Systems

"Alexandra H. Solomon delivers a beautifully relatable, encouraging, and practical book that walks the reader through the steps toward brave, intimate love. Her style creates safety and warmth from start to finish as she asks the readers to lean into vulnerability and connect with themselves in order to connect more deeply with others. *Loving Bravely* is a must-read for anyone interested in creating fulfilling and satisfying love while also transforming their relationships!"

—**Vienna Pharaon, LMFT**, founder of Mindful Marriage and
    Family Therapy in New York, NY, and relationship expert for
    Motherly

Loving Bravely

20 Lessons of Self-Discovery to Help You Get the Love You Want

Alexandra H. Solomon, PhD

New Harbinger Publications, Inc.

Publisher's Note

This publication is designed to provide accurate and authoritative information in regard to the subject matter covered. It is sold with the understanding that the publisher is not engaged in rendering psychological, financial, legal, or other professional services. If expert assistance or counseling is needed, the services of a competent professional should be sought.

Distributed in Canada by Raincoast Books

Copyright © 2017 by Alexandra H. Solomon
      New Harbinger Publications, Inc.
      5674 Shattuck Avenue
      Oakland, CA 94609
      www.newharbinger.com

Cover design by Amy Shoup; Text design by Michele Waters-Kermes; Acquired by Melissa Valentine; Edited by Erin Raber

---

Library of Congress Cataloging-in-Publication Data on file

19   18   17

10   9   8   7   6   5   4   3   2   1   First Printing

This book is dedicated to my most loving teachers:
Todd who teaches me about trust
Brian who teaches me about faith
Courtney who teaches me about joy
You are my world

And there you are
standing by
giving me space
to draw you close
conjuring
feeling and knowing
into touch
whispers
and light
on a page written
to the beat
of the very
you
that got me
here
we will make history
anew
dear Love
mastering
ourselves
in the midst
of each other
Loving Bravely

—(from "Dear Love" by Alexandra Folz)

Contents

Part 4: Self-Expansion

Foreword

Most of us love to be in love—but often we don't know how to find love or how to sustain it. In this remarkable book, Alexandra Solomon addresses both issues as she takes us on a journey of discovery, exploring the wonders, challenges, and dilemmas of love. *Loving Bravely* empowers the reader to shift from how to *find* Mr. or Ms. Right to how to *be* Mr. or Ms. Right. Alexandra identifies the key skills for being a great lover—not just in bed but also throughout the day. To be a great lover you need to develop "relational self-awareness"—understanding what makes you tick. Alexandra encourages us to examine our stories about love, sex, gender, and commitment. As she notes, these stories we tell ourselves shape our reactions, often in ways that leave us unhappy. Taking ownership of our own stories opens up a space for us to write a more successful narrative. In my own book I also explore the idea that, rather than being a victim in your life, you can be an author of your life and your relationship. Alexandra Solomon's book gives you a terrific roadmap for becoming the author of your own relational life.

Alexandra defines bravery as the courage to face yourself, to identify your vulnerabilities and ways of navigating in the relational world. To be brave in love is also to accept that love is messy and constantly evolving. Rather than thinking in black and white terms, she encourages us to embrace the gray area—to see the circularity of our dances with our partner and to embrace the dialectics of love. The same person who loves and protects us can let us down at times; we are kind and considerate, but we can be selfish and reactive when we feel threatened. Accepting the "both/and" nature of life and of love is part of the wisdom that Alexandra offers us.

In my work with distressed couples, I help them develop skills of "relational empowerment"—which includes emotion regulation, empathy, and generosity. Alexandra offers techniques that facilitate these skills. She suggests that we find a space between stimulus (when someone you love says things that upset you) and response (when you blow up at that person!). We don't have to react on automatic pilot, driven by our emotional brain. We can pause and ask, as Alexandra suggests, "What would love do?" We can respond with our higher brain, choosing a more mature response. Alexandra encourages us to examine how we "show up for love." In her view, we are not just passive recipients of what our partner dishes out. We can make choices that allow us to be successful lovers in the broadest sense.

The opening metaphor Alexandra uses in her introduction is of a driver in a car. This metaphor reappears in the book: she asks us, "Who's in the driver's seat of your life?" We could say that this book is a kind of Driver's Ed manual for your relational life. She offers this manual not in a cookbook kind of way—love can't be reduced to a bunch of how-tos. And she doesn't offer her ideas in a holier-than-thou preachy way. Alexandra Solomon offers her wisdom about relationships—and there is a lot of wisdom in this book—in an inviting, accessible, often funny way. In addition to referencing key ideas from psychology and relationship science, she shares vignettes from her clinical practice and from her own life. She is slogging through the same relational mud as the rest of us—and she invites us along on her own journey in the relational realm.

Love is not a destination; it is a process. To be a great lover, you need to develop skills of emotional intelligence. Alexandra offers us practical tools to develop these skills, along with ways to step outside of our own narrow beliefs and assumptions. She encourages us to develop authorship and freedom in our love lives.

You are in for a treat as you read this book. Alexandra's tone is witty, irreverent, and inviting. She understands the challenges of the current dating culture, as well as the ways we can get stuck in our own relational perspective based on our family history, culture, and gender training. In a delightful manner, Alexandra challenges us to name our assumptions and to grow so we can cultivate a more successful narrative. She encourages us to love ourselves so we can love another, and to bring self-compassion to our vulnerabilities. Go on the journey with her—you will come out wiser on the other side, with great tools to become the hero or heroine of your own love story.

—Mona DeKoven Fishbane, PhD
Author, *Loving with the Brain in Mind:*
Neurobiology and Couple Therapy
Director, Couple Therapy Training,
Chicago Center for Family Health

Introduction

The Love Classroom

If he desired to know about automobiles, he would, without question, study diligently about automobiles. If his wife desired to be a gourmet cook, she'd certainly study the art of cooking, perhaps even attending a cooking class. Yet, it never seems as obvious to him that if he wants to live in love, he must spend at least as much time as the auto mechanic or the gourmet in studying love.

—Leo Buscaglia

I remember the day I took my driving test at sixteen, sitting nervously at the DMV, frantically reviewing street signs in my head. I'd been preparing for more than a year. And while I had some trepidation about being trusted with this huge responsibility, I felt ready. Dammit, I had read the manual over and over and logged lots of practice time behind the wheel! When I plunged headfirst into a relationship with my husband, however, I had no such preparation. I didn't study for months about how to make a relationship last before leaning in for that first kiss. I didn't worry about the safety of my heart or his until years later when I already felt deeply invested. Why didn't I put the same due diligence into learning how to "do" love as I did into learning how to drive?

We assume that people ought to just know how to "do" love. And that is a huge problem. It's the very problem I have been addressing for almost twenty years in my therapy office, in my graduate teaching, and in an undergraduate course I teach at Northwestern University called "Building Loving and Lasting Relationships: Marriage 101." As you might imagine, this course is very popular and has received lots of media attention over the years because it is unique, which unfortunately reflects the fact that we have yet to figure out how to really value *relationship education*. Over the years, many people have told me that they *wished* they had had the chance to take a class like "Marriage 101" before committing to an intimate relationship.

What's worse is that those who are wise enough to seek a better understanding of themselves often end up feeling ashamed of themselves for doing so. I see this over and over in my clinical work. When an engaged couple comes to see me for premarital therapy, more often than not they begin our first session by making a self-conscious statement such as, "I can't believe we are doing couples therapy before we have even walked down the aisle." I quickly jump in and say that I wish all couples were so thoughtful and brave.

As a culture, we are obsessed with the *idea of love*—consider the $40 billion wedding industry and the entire genre of romance-based reality television. However, we are not nearly so obsessed with *investing in love*—note the divorce rate that hovers around 50 percent. All around us are people struggling in their intimate relationships, yet most of us are more than willing to enter into a committed intimate relationship or marriage with little or no preparation whatsoever.

Relational Self-Awareness

As I was preparing to write this book, I spent time reading popular books written for single people. Some offer tricks to "get" someone to fall in love with you: do this, say this. Others offer rules: don't text first, don't have sex for X number of dates. The message in most of these books seems to be: "If you listen to your intuition, you will screw it up and get hurt." I was cringing the whole time. I can certainly understand the wish for a recipe or a prescription—something to bring order to the confusion that love inevitably brings. But the problem with following somebody else's truth is that it puts you at risk of losing touch with your own. In this book, I will not tell you what to do or how to feel about your intimate relationship, but I will offer you the tools you need to make healthy and self-aware choices.

Connecting in an intimate way with someone else *must* start from within; it must come from a deep and courageous relationship with yourself. Loving somebody else requires us to be courageous, vulnerable, and real. And you cannot be real *with someone else* unless and until you can be real *with yourself.*

I don't believe you should simply wait around for that special someone to pop into your life. *I believe that your bravest and best work is to look at yourself, understand yourself, and grow yourself so that you can be that special someone.* I have seen this happen over and over with friends, with students, and with therapy clients. When we pay attention to and take responsibility for how we "do" love, we attract partners who are similarly curious, compassionate, and willing to be vulnerable. And we create intimate relationships that can go the distance—intimate relationships that value deep and authentic connection.

Self-awareness means knowledge of your own history, character, feelings, motives, and desires. This book is about *relational self-awareness:* understanding in a deep and heartfelt way how you "show up" for love. All the relationship tips, skills, and tools in the world will not add up to much unless they rest upon a foundation that is made up of your ongoing commitment to a brave, curious, and compassionate relationship with your own internal world. It will come as no surprise that relational self-awareness is at the heart of the "Marriage 101" course. Based on my many years of studying intimate relationships as a professor, couples therapist, and intimate partner, I can say with confidence: *relational self-awareness is the cornerstone of all healthy intimate relationships.*

Love Today

We expect much more from intimate relationships than we did fifty or one hundred years ago. Historically—and in many parts of the world today—love is not the foundation for marriage. In other times and other places, people married for economic, political, social, and familial reasons. Today, we expect our intimate partner to be our lover, best friend, confidant, coparent, and sometimes business partner. Some have argued that perhaps our divorce rate is so high because we actually have overburdened marriage with unrealistic and overly romantic expectations (Coontz 2006).

We are loving in the digital age, and we are just beginning to grasp the intricate ways that being plugged in affects how we love. Online dating apps create the illusion of endless choice, which can stir feelings of excitement as well as paralyzing anxiety. This virtual marketplace of love draws our attention outside of ourselves, putting us at greater risk than ever of believing that love is all about making the right choice. Certainly, choosing a compatible partner is one part of the equation. But it is just that—one part. All we can ever truly control is what we are bringing into a relationship.

In addition, scrolling social media day after day means that we are powerfully and subtly consuming other people's images and definitions of love. It is more difficult than ever to create and embody our own beliefs and values about love when we are flooded by everyone else's carefully edited and curated love stories. Given all the noise that is part of the digital age, relational self-awareness is more difficult than ever. And in order to be successful in love, *relational self-awareness is more important than ever.*

Brave Love

Quieting the noise and clearing the clutter allows us to deepen our relationship with ourselves. As we expand our relational self-awareness, we learn to trust ourselves and to pay attention to all the vital data that swirls within us. This shifts how we love our intimate partner. When relational self-awareness is our guiding principle, we realize that love is a classroom. Romantic love is one of the most powerful vehicles for self-transformation that we will ever encounter. As I tell my "Marriage 101" students, "Falling in love will grow your ass up!"

Viewing love as a classroom, ripe with opportunities to learn and grow, creates a shift within you. You begin to view your intimate partner as your teacher (and yourself as his or her teacher too). You see that everything that happens within your intimate relationship holds the possibility for personal transformation, and, from a place of curiosity and connection, you rise to the challenges of romantic love rather than fighting against them or running from them. Loving bravely means:

- Committing to the ongoing practice of relational self-awareness

- Understanding the stories you carry about love

- Accepting that there are no quick fixes or easy answers

- Striving for authenticity

- Being willing to look at your role in relationship challenges

- Seeing your partner as deeply connected to you and completely separate from you

- Viewing your differences as opportunities for growth rather than threats

- Seeking shades of gray, not black and white answers

- Feeling energized, rather than defeated, by the work of loving your partner

- Loving yourself because of, and not in spite of, your imperfections and tender spots

- Loving your partner because of, and not in spite of, his or her imperfections and tender spots

Loving like this is the work of a lifetime. As lovers, we are never done, fixed, or perfect. Nor would we want to be, as love thrives in the messy richness of *me, you,* and *us.* Brave love simply means that we commit ourselves to staying with the messy richness of love instead of ignoring it, suppressing it, or being crushed by it.

Whether you plan to marry or not, it is likely that intimate relationships are and will be central in your life. As mammals, the desire for intimate connection is woven into our DNA. I use the term "intimate relationship" because it is inclusive of a variety of stages and forms of relationships. The lessons in this book are relevant to any *type* of intimate relationship and any *stage* of intimate relationship development (dating, committed, living together, engaged, or married).

How to Use This Book

This book is a courageous journey within, offering twenty lessons that will grow your relational self-awareness so that you can love more bravely and deeply than ever before. These lessons are divided into four parts, each with its own intention:

Part 1: Self-Reflection. The intention is to learn how the past affects the present. We will gather answers to the questions: "What did I learn about love when I was growing up? How do my relationships with the people who raised me shape who I am in my intimate relationships?"

Part 2: Self-Awareness. The intention is to learn how cultural messages and cultural stories shape your beliefs about intimate relationships. We will gather answers to the questions: "What do I believe about love? How does that shape who I am in my intimate relationships?"

Part 3: Self-Expression. The intention is to learn how your relationship with your internal, emotional world affects you in your intimate relationship. We will gather answers to the questions: "How do I relate to my emotions? How does that shape who I am in my intimate relationships?"

Part 4: Self-Expansion. The intention is to solidify the path back to your deep and wise internal compass. We will gather answers to the questions: "How can I know when I have become lost from myself? How can I find my way back to a place that is authentic and whole?"

Although the lessons and exercises of the book are deeply personal, the possibilities for growth and transformation through the book can be supercharged by sharing your reflections and personal work in a group setting. You can find the "Loving Bravely: Reading Group Guide" online at http://www.newharbinger.com/35814.

The Name-Connect-Choose Process

As we journey through mind, body, heart, and spirit, our tool for expanding relational self-awareness is a process I call *Name-Connect-Choose*. You will practice this process throughout the book as we explore a variety of issues, topics, and questions. Change happens through the Name-Connect-Choose process:

- **Name** asks you to tell your story, identifying and declaring something as your truth or your experience. The power in naming comes from bringing what was buried (or out of your awareness) into the light for examination.

- **Connect** asks you to attune to yourself, turning your attention within and experiencing the emotions that are attached to the particular story you are telling. Connecting emotionally to your deep truth breathes life into your unearthed story.

- **Choose** asks you to take responsibility for how you love today. Whereas a lack of awareness inevitably keeps you stuck in a loop, conscious awareness facilitates choice. When you know more, you can make decisions from a place of eyes-open empowerment.

You can download a handout that reminds you how the Name-Connect-Choose process works at http://www.newharbinger .com/35814.

Steps Toward Loving Bravely

Each of the book's lessons is followed by a set of exercises that puts that lesson into practice in your life; they are called "Steps Toward Loving Bravely." These are journal-writing prompts, exercises, and practices designed to help you connect deeply with the work of the lesson, and they are integral to your growth. Completing the "Steps Toward Loving Bravely" will help you make the most of what this book has to offer.

Throughout the book, in order to better understand your intimate relationships, you will be asked to look at your relationship with the people who raised you. For the sake of simplicity, I will use the plural term "parents" throughout the book with full awareness of and respect for the many forms that families take. You may have grown up with two parents, or perhaps you had one parent, a relative, or others who served as caregivers for you. Your focus will be on the key adults who shaped your "love template"—the foundation of how you love today.

For readers who are currently in therapy, this book may open new avenues for you to explore with your therapist. For readers who are not in therapy, this book is likely to kick up some dust, so to speak. In fact, many of my students begin therapy during or after taking my courses, which is a very good thing! Exploring these topics in the safety of a therapeutic relationship can supercharge your relational self-awareness journey. I believe so much in the value of therapy that I have included information about how to find a therapist as appendix 2 at the end of this book.

Your Love Classroom

As a student, I always loved the first day of school. As a professor, I still love it! Every year, I stand in front of the students and say, "I am awestruck and grateful that we get to spend time together muddling through all the complexities of love. That's our job—to come together, share, study, question, and discover what it is we believe, individually and collectively, about love."

That is how I feel about this book as well! I am grateful to have the opportunity to explore with you in a deep, curious, personal way. As you travel through the pages of this book—your own love classroom—I hope your awareness expands and you grow more confident, competent, and brave in love. I can't tell you how to love, and I can't give you a recipe for success. Love is too personal and nuanced to obey any rulebook. What I *can* do is support and guide you through a journey that will open you up to your deepest truths. And I can promise that the work you will do in this book will grow your relational self-awareness, allowing you to make vital and healing shifts in your relationship to yourself and to your intimate partner.

PART 1

Self-Reflection

Lesson 1

Understand Your Past

*Do the best you can until you know better. Then when you know
better, do better.*

—Maya Angelou

You exist in the present moment, with your past behind you and
your future ahead of you. But your past is still with you—and always
will be—and it shapes the lens through which you experience the
present moment. **Your past shapes how you love.**

The family you grew up in granted you your first relationship
curriculum. Your family home was your first love classroom. In that
classroom, you were offered lessons about how to give and receive
love, how to handle difference and conflict, and how to ask for your
needs to be met. Your *attachment style*—an alchemical blend of
nature and nurture that dictated how you reached for and connected
with your caregivers—was in place before your second birthday.
And, in all likelihood, that attachment style remains with you today.
How you reached for and connected with your caregivers is probably
a lot like how you reach for and connect with your intimate partner
today. **The past comes with us.**

The relationship that your parents had with each other was your
first template for an intimate relationship. This is true regardless of
the structure and quality of that relationship: intact and loving,
intact but unhealthy, or severed. The relationship between your
parents was your first love template even if they never had an intimate relationship with each other—the absence of something can

still have an impact. How the adults in your life navigated their intimate relationships taught you about love. Some of the learning was explicit; most of it was implicit.

In the opening scene of the 2015 movie *Trainwreck*, Amy Schumer's character is a little girl sitting with her sister on the hood of the family station wagon. Their father, by way of explaining the impending divorce, asks the girls to repeat after him, again and again, "Monogamy isn't realistic." That was some seriously explicit teaching about love! Most of our parents more subtly offered us messages about what to expect and not expect from an intimate relationship, and we took in a great deal by listening, watching, and feeling how our parents loved.

Did your parents demonstrate compassion, tenderness, respect, and honesty in their intimate relationship(s)? If so, you probably aspire to bring those elements into your love life, as well. Did your parents demonstrate hostility, abuse, addiction, neglect, or deceit? If so, you probably aspire to break the chain and love differently than what you were shown. Unfortunately, just saying, "I'll never end up like my parents" is not enough because many, if not most, of the messages about love that we internalize in childhood, though impactful, are quiet and out of our direct awareness. There's a big difference between talking the talk and walking the walk. Family patterns, loyalties, and legacies are strong, and unless you are willing to explore your past, you are at risk of having old patterns in the driver's seat of your love life, rather than you.

No Enemies Within

It can feel frightening to explore the past. Even my graduate students resist digging up their ancient history because it is uncomfortable, unsettling, and painful. But they must do so in order to become competent therapists. Think about that—these are people who are choosing to dedicate their lives to family dynamics and yet they are hesitant to explore their own! You are not alone in your fear!

Many of us prefer to believe that just saying "the past is the past" makes it so. I get it. After all, what if the past was full of pain and dysfunctional relationships? And what if it means that you are therefore incapable of love? Fortunately, I firmly believe that nobody is damaged beyond repair. Healing is always possible. I have seen people who grew up in really dysfunctional families go on to become generous and devoted partners and parents. A healthy intimate relationship is always possible—as long as both partners are deeply committed to checking themselves when the past sneaks into the present, as it always does. This isn't just a onetime exercise—it's a lifestyle.

During a discussion in the "Marriage 101" course about the dysfunctional family patterns surrounding addiction, infidelity, and domestic violence, one of my students, Lena, raised her hand looking worried. "All three of those things happened in the family I grew up in," she said. "Does that mean I'm doomed to fail in my intimate relationship?" My answer was a resounding *no!* The fact that her *family of origin*—the family she grew up in—struggled in these ways does not mean that she is doomed to repeat unhealthy patterns, but it does mean that she has the responsibility (and opportunity!) to explore the impact that these patterns had on her. ***Awareness facilitates choice.***

This notion really hit home for me when I was attending a workshop given by Dr. Terrence Real, who described it this way: "Family dysfunction is like fire in the woods that rolls generation to generation taking everything in its path until one person has the courage to face the flame. That person brings peace to her ancestors and spares those who follow." Those of us who grew up in families that struggled to love with integrity and wholeness *can* break these patterns. Dr. Real's words touched me deeply because they reminded me to reframe my own healing journey. When I think about the many hours I have spent in my own therapy and with my husband in couples therapy, I risk feeling flooded with shame about my "brokenness." What helps is for me to become aware of how I negatively talk to myself ("What is wrong with you?") and then to shift my perspective by remembering that I can feel proud of my deep commitment to breaking unhealthy family patterns, some of which go back multiple generations. Feelings of shame transform as I instead take comfort in my dedication to living wholeheartedly (Brown 2015).

If you want or need to be the person who has the courage to face the flames, the work you do with this book will help you chart a new course. Being honest about your past makes it much more likely that you will be able to enjoy a happy and healthy intimate relationship today and in the future. Relational self-awareness is not only essential for your intimate relationship, it is also essential if you plan to become a parent (or if you already are one). Dr. Dan Siegel (2013) explains that "making sense of your life is important because it supports your ability to provide emotionally connecting and flexible relationships with your children" (38–39).

The Way Out Is Through

My student, Lena, voiced a legitimate concern. Unless she heals the parts of herself that were hurt by the unhealthy dynamics in her family, she is at risk of choosing a partner who is reminiscent of one or both of her parents, and she is at risk of behaving like one or both of her parents. In an unconscious effort to heal old wounds, we tend to fall in love with partners who are either very similar to our parents *or* the exact opposite of our parents. Either path fans the flames. Lena might be drawn to a man who is abusive like her father or a man who is submissive and voiceless like her mother. She might tolerate someone's unfaithful behavior because she believes this is the best she can expect from a man. She might behave dishonestly or violently herself from a belief that it is better to be the perpetrator than the victim.

Or she can grow her relational self-awareness and chart a new course. Her course. Putting out the fire and refusing to re-create what she saw and experienced growing up will require her to engage in what I call the *Name-Connect-Choose* process. This process is our tool of change, expanding our relational self-awareness about how the past affects our intimate relationships today.

Name: Call the past what it is with honesty about how you were or are impacted.

Connect: Allow yourself to feel the impact of the past without judgment.

Choose: Consciously choose love again and again.

Name

This first step—naming family dynamics—requires you to be *brave*. It can feel disloyal to name your mother's alcoholism. It can feel humiliating to name your father's infidelity. It can feel frightening to name your brother's suicide. Yet, those experiences, for better or for worse, are with you today. When they remain unnamed, they are in the driver's seat of your love life, shaping your relationship choices. When you name them, you take a step toward putting yourself in the driver's seat.

Connect

This second step—feeling the impact without judgment—requires you to go *deep*. It's so easy to judge ourselves out of feelings about the past: "My mom's drinking wasn't that bad. What's the big deal?" I am in no way advocating that we travel to and then stay stuck in the past, as that turns us into victims. But the reality is that most of us hang out at the other extreme: refusing to allow ourselves to grieve and feel the full weight of old hurt. As therapists often say, "The way out is through."

Choose

This third step becomes available when your expanded awareness allows you to choose a path of more *intimate* connection with your partner. This path is possible for you even if you were raised by people who were not able to honor themselves or their relationship with each other in this way. Committing to honoring your relationship with *yourself* as the precursor for your relationship with everyone else means being willing to curiously ask yourself questions like:

> In what ways am I being held back by beliefs and stories that do not serve me?

> In what ways am I feeling and acting from a place of old wounds?

> What can I do to shift to a place of empowerment?

Relational Self-Awareness in Action: Becoming Instead of Seeking

What happens when you surrender the belief that the key to a successful intimate relationship is finding Mr. or Ms. Right, and you instead deeply trust that the key to a successful intimate relationship is *becoming and being* Mr. or Ms. Right? Ask twenty-six-year-old Alexia. I have been doing therapy with Alexia for several years. Her parents divorced when she was twelve, and she is a member of two very complicated blended families. She has been in several intimate relationships with guys during the course of our work together. At first, she was blind to her role in any relationship dynamic. Her story was simply that there was something wrong with him: He wasn't affectionate enough. He was too clingy. He had no ambition. He worked too many hours.

As we worked together to make sense of her past—looking closely at the lessons she learned from her family of origin about intimacy and conflict—she slowly began to widen her lens, seeing how patterns from the past shape her experiences in her relationships today.

Now she has a different approach in her current relationship. Instead of focusing exclusively on what her partner is doing "wrong," she watches herself. Now, when she finds herself feeling reactive and critical of her boyfriend, the first thing she does is turn inward so that she can have an honest and gentle dialogue with *herself*. Again and again, she commits to taking a curious stance vis-à-vis herself, wondering whether and how her responses to the present-moment reality with her boyfriend are being shaped by old stories from her past.

This does not mean that she blames herself when things go "wrong." And it does not mean that she simply bites her tongue when she feels annoyed and frustrated, assuming it must be just her old issues acting up again. Not at all. But it does mean that Alexia respects that she is a huge part of the equation. She knows that the dynamics in an intimate relationship are *always* made up of "your stuff," "my stuff," and "our stuff." Taking responsibility for her "stuff"—the impact of her family dynamics on her thoughts, feelings, and beliefs about love—helps her ask for what she needs from an empowered place rather than a blaming place. She is learning to be Ms. Right, and her current relationship is her happiest one yet.

Steps Toward Loving Bravely

The experiences you had when you were growing up shape how you think about, feel about, and behave in your intimate relationships today.

Then and Now

Write words or phrases that capture the nature or personality of each of the people who raised you (for example, short-tempered, affectionate, opinionated, easygoing, full of energy). Next, write words or phrases that capture the nature or personality of the last two or three people you dated. Finally, place the descriptions side by side. What do you notice? What are the similarities? What are the differences?

Take note of how you feel as you do this exercise. Are you aware of feeling invested in it going a certain way or yielding a certain outcome? If so, notice that and try to approach the exercise as a detective or an anthropologist—in other words, with greater distance and neutrality—trusting that brave exploration paves the way to healthier and deeper intimate connections.

Brave Choices in Action

Write down three aspects of your family life that felt precious, beneficial, and valuable to you when you were growing up (for example, I appreciate that my father's face lit up when my siblings or I entered the room; I appreciate that my mother valued family meals; I appreciate that my family had inside jokes and lots of humor).

Also write down three aspects of your family life that felt destructive, hurtful, and/or unhelpful (for example, My family rarely said "I love you"; my parents handled their feelings by raging and/or shutting down; my parents lied to each other).

These lists will reveal the beliefs, values, patterns, and traditions that you want to carry on in your own life, as well as the ones that you are probably eager to leave behind. The process of identifying what you admire and what troubles you about your family dynamics will go a long way toward helping you create a healthy and happy intimate relationship. The work of this book will support your efforts to embody what you value and let go of what does not serve you in your intimate relationship.

Lesson 2

Craft Your Story

When you can look a thing dead in the eye, acknowledge that it exists, call it exactly what it is, and decide what role it will take in your life, then, my beloved, you have taken the first step toward your freedom

—Iyanla Vanzant

Ten months ago, Mark and Tonya sat in my office crying, their heads heavy in their hands. They wept tears of sadness *and* relief. At least everything was finally on the table. Although their marriage had been leveled, they could glimpse possibilities for rebuilding. The shame, rage, and fear Mark had been carrying for years had simply become too much, so over a stretch of exhausting days, he revealed to Tonya layer after layer of truths that he had kept hidden deep within. He confessed to having multiple affairs—affairs Tonya had long suspected without confirmation. He also revealed that as an adolescent he had been sexually abused by a teacher. Tonya's heart was broken. She hurt everywhere as she learned what Mark went through years ago, and she was full of rage and sadness about his dishonest behavior in the marriage.

Today the relationship between Mark and Tonya is the strongest it has been. Mark is devoted to his recovery. Before his world crashed around him, he was a *victim*. In addition to acting out sexually, he was prone to fits of rage, quickly blaming Tonya for the problems in the marriage and unable to look at his own behavior. He is now a *survivor*. He stands honestly in his story—the story of his abuse, the story of his inappropriate and wildly hurtful actions, and the story of his healing. He is by no means perfect, as that is never the goal. But he is honest, and he is brave. He takes responsibility for the relationship challenges that resulted from his trauma (difficulties with trust and feeling close), which means that he no longer unfairly blames his wife. Tonya is healing as well. At first she felt that staying in the marriage was a sign of weakness, but as she claimed much-needed time and space to focus on herself, she unearthed her deepest truth: wanting to stay and see what is possible within the marriage. She began working to forgive Mark and asking for what she needs from him in order to rebuild trust.

Not every couple could (or should) survive a chapter like this, but Mark and Tonya are buoyed by a deep commitment to the life they built together and a belief that "the way out is through."

The Power of Story

Doing couples therapy with Mark and Tonya reminds me of *the power of story*—how much healing is possible when we bravely claim the stories of our lives and stand without shame in our truth. Storytelling yields understanding within a person and between people. There is a branch of psychology called *personality psychology*, and researchers in this field take a variety of approaches to understanding a person. Some personality psychologists say that personality is a collection of relatively stable traits like introversion, extroversion, neuroticism, and agreeableness. Other personality psychologists say that if you want to know someone, you need to know his or her life story. According to these folks, *our life story is our personality*. They say that we are our life story. They say that the best way to truly know a person is to know the story they tell about the life they live.

I have loved this storytelling approach to psychology since I first learned about it twenty-plus years ago, and honoring the power of story has served me in the classroom, in my therapy office, and in my own self-awareness journey. It means that instead of looking for symptoms or problems or what's "wrong" with clients, I opt to bear witness as they weave together the moments of their journey thus far. It means that together we explore how their stories are serving them and how their stories are getting in their way. Our stories have a huge impact on how we feel about ourselves and our intimate relationships.

Think about the elements of a story. A story has a *plot*, events that happen in a sequence across time. A story has *characters*, usually a main character or narrator and a variety of supporting characters. A story has a *setting*, a context in which everything takes place. Beyond these basics, what we expect and desire is for a story to *make sense*. We like stories to have coherence and cohesiveness, holding together and flowing through time and space. Now think about your life story. Your life is a series of events (or chapters) that have taken place over time, in a variety of settings, with key others who impact and are impacted by you. **The events of your life are dots, and how you connect them illuminates and creates your very self.** The stories you tell about your life reflect all the messages you have internalized (from yourself, family, friends, and culture) about *who* you are in the world as well as messages about *how* the world works. How you cast yourself in the scenes and chapters of your story reflects what you have been told implicitly and explicitly about who you are. Are you a hero? A villain? A victim? A warrior? A damsel in distress? A survivor?

Research shows that *how* we tell the story of our lives is more meaningful than *what* actually happens to us. The tone and quality of the stories we tell about ourselves and our relationships say a lot about who we are. How we fit the events in our lives together reflects and shapes our outlook on life. How we tell our story affects how we interact with the world around us. Those of us whose life stories include blessings, goodness, and hope—even within sad and painful chapters—tend to live with more happiness and peace of mind. Those whose life stories are fragmented, incoherent, and thin tend to struggle to connect deeply with self and others (McAdams 2006).

Your life story affects how you connect with those around you, so creating a life story that is coherent and cohesive is a key aspect of relational self-awareness.

The great news about our stories is that we are always in charge of them. We are the authors! And, when we are willing to bravely explore how we are living within our life story, we open the possibility to change course. This doesn't mean denying or minimizing painful events in the service of writing a fairy tale. But it may mean that the first step toward greater empowerment, authenticity, and wholeness is becoming aware that early events in your life led you to be cast in a role that no longer serves you.

Life Creates Core Issues...

This shift toward greater empowerment, authenticity, and wholeness is the essence of Mark's transformation. Mark had habitually cast himself in the role of a helpless victim in the story of his life. Plot lines were all about his need to keep his guard up to protect himself from others who were out to get him. This *is* indeed an accurate portrayal of the chapter in his life during which he was abused. He was in danger and he was not protected. Yet this traumatic chapter cast an enormous shadow on every other chapter of his story, leading him to connect the dots in his life in a way that reflected and perpetuated his victim stance. Haunted by a past he didn't know how to face, he unthinkingly but vigilantly scanned the world for potential danger: His boss was going to betray him any day now, and his wife was deceitful and controlling. This lens skewed his perspective, created tremendous internal fear, and deeply compromised his ability to love. (For more about the impact of trauma, see appendix 1.)

Even without a trauma history like Mark's, each and every one of us has negative themes that recur in our life stories. Let's call these negative themes our *core issues*. A core issue is a vulnerability, a tender spot. It is a wound in need of healing—or at the very least, a still-tender scar. Core issues are sometimes called our shadow, our emotional allergies, or our emotional blind spots. Our core issues tend to hang just outside of our conscious awareness, leading us to mistake our perceptions for absolute Truth.

When we are unaware of our core issues or when we avoid or ignore them, we actually fuel our core issues and give them power. As the opening quote by Iyanla Vanzant reveals, looking your core issues in the eye and calling them what they are defuses them and allows *you* (not your pain, not your past) to be in charge of your life. I believe 100 percent in something that family therapists call the *health premise* (Pinsof 1995). The health premise is the idea that we are healthy until proven otherwise, and we are inherently worthy, good, and whole. Sometimes, usually because we are in pain, we behave in ways that are forgetful and do not honor that which we truly are. In other words, our natural state is supportive of connection and love (love of self *and* love of others). We learn hate, we learn fear, and we learn mistrust. Keeping the health premise in mind can reduce our resistance to looking at our core issues, as doing so helps us remember that we are deeply okay even as we look at parts of ourselves that feel messy and very much not okay.

When we don't take the time to identify our specific tender spots, we are essentially stuck in an old story—one that may have accurately described the past but that doesn't belong in the present. Being stuck means we are at risk of moving through the world with little awareness and even less control over our internal, emotional landscape. We are at risk of unfairly blaming others. We are at risk of feeling repeatedly like a victim. When Mark was stuck replaying his old story of pain and betrayal, he couldn't show up for his relationship with Tonya. Showing up means being present and taking full responsibility for ourselves.

...Intimate Relationships Stir Them Up

In all my years as a therapist, I have yet to meet a core issue that does not invoke my compassion and empathy. Core issues come from life experience, from the "nurture" aspect of the nature-nurture formula. Core issues can be created by experiences in your family of origin, experiences in school, experiences with friends, and/or relationship experiences.

Core issues can also be created by elements of your cultural identity intersecting with your life experiences. For example, an African American man growing up in the United States may identify a core issue of pervasive mistrust because of feedback he has received from the world around him based on the color of his skin. He may develop this core issue *even if* he grew up in a home where his parents provided an atmosphere of emotional safety and security. Similarly, a woman who identifies as lesbian may find herself struggling with a core issue of defectiveness because of societal messages she received about what it means to be gay.

Regardless of the origin of your core issues, one thing is for sure. Your core issues *will* get stirred up again and again in your intimate relationships. You have no control over that. It is the very nature of love. What you do have control over is how you respond when your intimate relationship invites you into deep, close contact with your tender spots. For example, Suzanne has a pattern of not being able to get past a first date with new women, and her story each time is that her date "says something stupid that's a turnoff." It is entirely possible that Suzanne keeps meeting Ms. Wrong. But I would invite her to *entertain* the hypothesis that this pattern reflects a core issue within her, and that her story about herself and the world around her is getting in her way.

- Perhaps she is afraid of being judged harshly, so she judges others first.

- Perhaps she is afraid of getting left behind, so she leaves first.

- Perhaps she is full of negative self-talk, so she is as critical of others as she is of herself.

Transforming this pattern and getting to a second date requires her to bravely examine how the story she is telling herself is getting in her way.

Willingness to stand honestly within our story takes guts. Tempting as it may be to omit chapters with pain, disappointment, and cruelty, doing so compromises our relationship with ourselves and therefore our relationship with others, including an intimate partner. Working to create a coherent and cohesive life story is healing. It also shines a light on negative themes, or core issues. You will begin to identify your core issues here and continue the work in later lessons as well. Owning our core issues moves us from passive to active, from victim to survivor, deepening our capacity to love.

Steps Toward Loving Bravely

How you tell the story of your life shapes how you live and how you love. Learn your old story so you can choose to make it anew.

The Story of Your Life

Create a table of contents for the story of your life. Ask yourself:

What is the title of your life story?

How will you divide the chapters?

What will you title those chapters?

The intention of this exercise is twofold. Working with the story of your life in this way can help you bring to light the major themes that are at play in your life. In addition, the very process of working with your life story creates narrative coherence, which is healing.

Filling in the Details

As you create your table of contents, add some detail and richness to it by answering the following questions:

Who are the major characters? Think of the people who have stood in your corner as well as those who have presented you with battles and challenges.

As you look at your chapter titles and think about those chapters, what would you say are the central conflicts or major themes in your life? For example, you may notice a pattern of falling down but getting back up. Or you may notice a theme of all good things come to an end. Or you may notice a theme about the importance of community or the importance of achievement.

What have been your most impactful lessons so far? For example, learning to stand up for yourself in relationships with authority figures or learning to love again after a heartbreak.

What are the *turning points*—times when something decisively changed for you? You might not have called it such at the time, but now when you look back you may be able to see that life before and life after are quite different. For example, quitting smoking or going back to school. What does that turning point say about you?

What are your favorite chapters and why?

In what ways have you been blessed?

Take a little time to connect with yourself: How did it feel to work with your life story? What surprised you about the process?

Next Chapters

As the author of your life story, your voice is everything. This final exercise will help you become and remain an empowered author. Select three to five overarching words or themes that capture the chapters of your life story so far. Some themes may be positive (resilience, setting and reaching goals, and so forth), but some may be negative, pointing you to your core issues. Next, write down three to five words or themes that you would like to have capture the *upcoming* chapters of your life story—your *upcoming chapter themes*. Put these two lists—your core issues and your upcoming chapter themes—side by side, and take note of the changes you are hoping to make. It might be helpful to frame these changes as *shifts*: "Shifting from _____ to _____ ." If you prefer images to words, you could paint, draw, or create a collage that captures what you would like to bring into your life going forward.

Lesson 3

Awaken to Your Life Today

Realize deeply that the present moment is all you have. Make the Now the primary focus of your life.

—Eckhart Tolle

Your *story* has a past, a present, and a future, but your *life* is lived in this moment. As humans, our ability to reflect on the past and dream of the future is a bit of a double-edged sword. Yes, mental time travel has its benefits. We can reminisce as a way to feel close to those in our lives, and we can look ahead in order to make plans and create goals. But there is a dark side to focusing on the past or the future. It is difficult to feel happy and connected to others if we are habitually leaving the present moment by rewinding or fast-forwarding inside our heads. When our thoughts take us to the past, we tend to experience shame and blame. When our thoughts take us to the future, we tend to experience anxiety and self-doubt. Living in the present moment is our best chance for happiness and peace of mind. And living in the present moment helps us in love.

Living well, with an open heart that is loving of self and loving of others, requires bringing ourselves, again and again, as fully as possible, into the present moment—and that means knowing how to work with our stories. While we need to acknowledge and honor the impact that the past has on us today, we also need to be careful not to get stuck there. Spiritual teacher and author Carolyn Myss says, "By remaining stuck in the power of our wounds, we block our own transformation. We overlook the greater gifts inherent in our wounds—the strength to overcome them and the lessons we are meant to receive through them. Wounds teach us to become passionate and wise" (1997, 15). When you import into the present moment old, outdated, and inaccurate stories about who you are and how the world works, there are two unfortunate consequences:

- Your intimate relationship is compromised, because your view of the present moment is being skewed by the past.

- You are prevented from honoring the resilience and wisdom that emerges from pain—resilience and wisdom that in fact can serve you and your intimate relationship right here, right now.

In this lesson we will talk about how to live in the here and now of your life by working gently and lovingly with old stories that have a way of sneaking up on us.

Ghosts from the Past

Leticia and Owen showed up to our weekly therapy session wanting to rehash yet another explosive fight—a fight in which each of them felt very much like the victim. Here's what had happened: Owen had agreed to pick Leticia's car up from the mechanic, but he was swamped at work and forgot to get it. The next morning, when Leticia headed out to the garage, she was surprised that it wasn't waiting there for her, and she ended up being late for an appointment. She called Owen and unleashed her fury. She called him names, attacked his character (calling him lazy, dishonest, phony, and worthless), and she threatened to end the relationship. The more she attacked him, the more he defended himself, and each of them felt hurt, angry, and deeply misunderstood.

Although Leticia's upset was certainly understandable, it felt out of proportion to the situation. I suspected that something else was going on for her—something from her past—and I very gently said to her, "Leticia, I get how frustrating this incident with Owen was and is for you. And I can't get past this nagging sense that something very old is going on for you. Something that has nothing to do with the successful and ambitious woman sitting in this room today and everything to do with the little girl you once were. In that moment in the garage, when Owen's forgetfulness disappointed you so severely, I suspect something much deeper was getting stirred up in you."

Tears filled her eyes (and Owen's eyes, too), and she began to talk about her past in a way she never had done before. As the only child of a single mother, she and her mother were extremely close. Her mother was (and is) hardworking and driven. She was also prone to fits of rage; she would explode at Leticia's slightest misstep, calling her names and hitting her. Leticia never told anyone and maintained a very split view of her mother (loving mom/angry mom). She had so many reasons *not* to talk about the past. She feared it would change Owen's view of her mother. She feared Owen might use it against her down the road. She feared it might keep her from being able to have a relationship with her mother today. But part of her, a resilient and wise part, knew the past was haunting her.

When Leticia would fly into a rage, Owen felt as though a switch had flipped, and he was dealing with a different person. And in many ways, he was. During a fight, it's as if Leticia "becomes" that terrified little girl and Owen "becomes" the unpredictable mother. In those moments, Leticia is living in the past, desperately fighting a ghost, and both of them are lost. Leticia is lost within an old and painful story, and Owen is lost in confusion and fear. But her willingness to be vulnerable with him by sharing the past opened the door to a brand-new, brave, and deep intimacy between them. He was able to feel and express tremendous empathy for the girl she was. To him, it was like putting a missing piece into a puzzle.

Embracing Both/And

Leticia needed to let her guard down in order to talk with us about the pain of her childhood. She trusted Owen enough (although just barely) to share the truth of her past with him. Also, a part of her was tired of living like this. Even though she would defend and justify her behavior by blaming Owen for "making" her mad, she was sick of being triggered so easily, and her rageful behavior confused and frightened her. Changing this old pattern is hard work because it means she must face her past and tackle her core issues.

In order to be able to do what she did in session—in order to take responsibility for her relational behavior—she had to be able to take a *dialectic approach*. Dialectics is the core of a powerful therapeutic approach created by Dr. Marsha Linehan called dialectical behavior therapy (2015). Dialectics is a complex concept that has its roots in philosophy and science, and it involves several assumptions about the nature of reality: 1) everything is connected to everything else; 2) change is constant and inevitable; and 3) opposites can be integrated to form a closer approximation of the truth (which is always evolving). The last point has particular significance in learning to love bravely. Let's look at some examples:

I feel *both* excited *and* afraid.

This moment is full of *both* joy *and* sadness.

I am *both* feminine *and* athletic.

I can be *both* rational *and* emotional.

My partner is *both* whole *and* a work in progress.

Both my point of view *and* my partner's point of view make sense.

Thinking and acting dialectically can be quite difficult to do, downright impossible at times. The ability to move to this "both/and" thinking is vital for individual well-being and for relational happiness. Dialectics help us expand our ways of considering a situation. They can "unstick" conflicts by reducing blame and increasing flexibility and compassion. For Leticia, holding the dialectical view—Owen disappointed me *and* Owen cares deeply about me—has helped her begin to more effectively handle moments when pain from the past comes rushing in. In this both/and space, she can honor her emotions while also honoring the relationship. A dialectical approach in the face of a conflict does not mean giving up your values or selling out—it means acknowledging the truth on both sides.

If you find yourself prone to all-or-nothing, good-or-bad, right-or-wrong thinking, dialectics offer a new way. And when it comes to love, being able to hold dialectics is key. Nothing on Earth quite compares to the vulnerability invoked within an intimate relationship. And when we feel vulnerable, we are at risk of seeking what is simple and concrete in an attempt to steady ourselves. Black or white, good or bad, right or wrong are simple and concrete for sure. But they are usually far too narrow to hold the complexity and paradox of an intimate relationship.

Leticia, in a desperate effort to keep the past in the past, held an extremely rigid view of who she was—successful, ambitious, determined, and sure of herself. Her erratic and rage-filled behavior with Owen didn't fit within her narrow self-definition, so she did two things:

- She pushed those awful moments out of her awareness, acting minutes later as if it never happened (and insisting Owen do the same).

- She blamed those awful moments on Owen ("I yelled because of *his* behavior").

When Leticia didn't see her car in the garage, deep feelings of fear and worthlessness were *triggered*, or stirred up, within her: "Owen forgot me!" Without a dialectical approach, the old story was in charge, and her fear quickly became rage. As she becomes better able to embrace complexity, she can author a new story: "I feel both angry *and* sad. Owen loves me *and* he forgot to take care of something for me."

As she courageously named her story of herself and her past, she began to connect with and honor the terrified girl that she was. She softened and widened her view of herself, adding complexity and nuance. Her story became thicker and richer, allowing her to feel *both* successful, ambitious, determined, and sure of herself *and* frightened, needy, and unsure. Both/and. One does not destroy the other. Ever. One does not lessen the other. Ever.

Bravery and humility are required in order to say, "My internal world is complex and mysterious. The experiences in my life reveal new layers of myself to me. I can look without judgment at what bubbles up within me, trusting that I can experience the fullness of what it is to be me." Naming the old story and connecting to it sets the stage for Leticia to be able to choose different behaviors in her relationship. She can advocate for herself and her needs in her relationship with Owen without tearing him to shreds in the process.

Parenting Yourself from the Inside

Old, rigid, either/or stories don't stand a chance in the face of complex, nuanced, juicy stories of the self and of the relationship. Being able to find an internal both/and space opens up the possibility for *self-soothing*. Because how we relate to ourselves determines everything about how we relate to other people, self-soothing is actually a vital relationship skill. I like to think of self-soothing as becoming a parent to yourself because when we soothe ourselves, we offer comfort to ourselves the way a parent offers comfort to an upset child (Siegel and Hartzel 2013; Fishbane 2013).

Here's a personal example of self-soothing in the form of parenting yourself. I was about to give an important talk. It wasn't my biggest audience ever, but it was an intimidating one—full of former professors, colleagues, and strangers. And the topic, spirituality, was a new one for me. It felt like a big risk, and I was really nervous. On the drive to the venue, I tried my usual preparation routine of cranking up my favorite Jay-Z song—the one that gets me in the zone. It did *nothing* to calm my nerves. I started to get a little panicky. My heart was racing, I was getting sweaty, and my hands were clammy. My thoughts were all over the place: *What if I freak out on stage? What if I make a fool of myself?*

After a few minutes of running myself ragged, part of me rose above the fray and was able to see what was happening from a little distance. This part of me was saying, "These are all *stories*. These are just old stories. You don't need them." Naming the fact that I was having some stressful thoughts allowed me to begin to shift from panic to compassion. Next, I imagined myself as a kid. I literally pictured my round face and thick curly hair. I imagined talking to my younger self the way a scared kid needs to be talked to. I validated the girl's feelings ("You're scared right now, aren't you?"). I imagined giving her a hug and patting her curls. Then I reminded her that actually *she* wasn't the one who was going to stand in front of all those people. Giving the talk was the job of a woman, not a girl. She could play or rest or just generally be a kid. I, the woman, would give this talk. And I, the woman, had everything I needed to get the job done.

Guess what? It worked like a charm. I calmed right down, and I was able to do what needed to be done. Although this example doesn't directly involve my intimate relationship, I assure you that being able to parent myself from within creates a steady platform from which I can connect to my partner. The same is true for you.

Awakening to your life today means honoring the fact that you may be haunted from time to time by old stories that no longer serve you. Naming those old stories when they impinge on the present moment requires humility and awareness. Connecting with the impact of those old stories opens the door to compassion with self. And, most important, turning inward and attending to the impact of the past on the present moment facilitates choice. We can remain the victims of our old stories—reactive, stuck, and narrow—or we can soften, open, and parent ourselves from within. The latter path adds complexity and nuance to a dried-out old story. From a both/ and place of compassion, intimate connection with others can flow.

Steps Toward Loving Bravely

Clarity about the impact of the past on your life today allows you to parent yourself from the inside—relating to yourself with wisdom and compassion so that you can love fully in the here and now.

Being Here Now

One of the best ways to get better at living in the present moment is to practice *mindfulness*. Being mindful simply means bringing your attention to the present moment without judgment. As with most things in life, the more we practice, the better we get! You may find it helpful to take several two- or three-minute *mindfulness breaks* throughout the day, for example when you sit down to a meal, when you park your car at work in the morning, and/or when you are in the shower. Or you might enjoy doing one longer daily mindfulness meditation. There are lots of great books, audio recordings, and apps devoted to teaching mindfulness. Here are some tips:

Sit comfortably.

As you sit, still and quiet, scan your body, bringing your attention to each part of your body, from head to toes. Take note of the various sensations you are experiencing.

Focus on your breath, noticing how it feels in your nose, mouth, chest, and belly.

As thoughts bounce around inside your head, return your focus to your breath. I find it helpful to imagine that my present-moment awareness is a blue sky and each thought inside my head is a cloud. When a thought comes in, I note it and allow it to pass on by like the cloud, as I return my attention to the sky—my present-moment awareness of my breath. You will probably need to do this over and over again.

Mindfulness meditation takes practice, but the benefits to your physical and emotional well-being—as well as your romantic relationship—are worth it!

Parenting Yourself Today

Find a place in your home to post a photo of yourself as a child. Having that photo in view can serve as a reminder to relate to yourself with compassion. When you notice yourself engaging in unhelpful and unkind stories about who you are ("You can't do anything right! No wonder you are single. You are fat, lazy, weak!"), look at that photo and imagine talking to your younger self in that way. You wouldn't, would you? Ask yourself, "What does that kid need to hear instead?"

Forge a New Connection

When you parent, it's crucial you realize you aren't raising a "mini-me," but a spirit throbbing with its own signature.

—Shefali Tsabary

From the moment we are born until we take our last breath, we are always changing, yet it is easy for us to retain a perspective of our parents or caregivers that we created when we were kids. Clinging to an old story of who they are can negatively affect your love life. Through the lens of an out-of-date story, your parents are stuck in the past, and, more important, *you* are stuck in the past. It is important to "grow up" your relationship with your parents and to get to know them as the people they are today. And to get to know them as the person *you* are today. *Forging a mature adult relationship with your parents is essential because an outdated story can keep you from making healthy choices in your intimate relationships.*

Fresh Data

We know that the past has a huge impact on our love lives, and we know there is a strong connection between our original *love template* (the relationship models we saw when we were growing up) and our intimate relationships today. Therefore, this entire lesson is devoted to helping you love more consciously by collecting *fresh data*. In other words, you are being invited and encouraged to talk about love with the people who raised you. The intention of talking to your parents is threefold:

- It will help you more deeply understand your love template.

- It will help you better understand who they are *today* and how that is different from who they were when you were young.

- It will help them get to know *you* as you are today.

Regardless of your age or relationship status, the process of seeking fresh data from your parents and offering fresh data to your parents about *your* life will grow relational self-awareness.

I believe in this so much that in both of the courses I teach, I have my students do it! We call it a *parent interview*. The transformation that comes from this assignment is unlike anything else in my teaching. Even though this assignment often invokes a full spectrum of reactions from enthusiasm and curiosity to fear and dread, year after year students inevitably come away from the experience feeling grateful, optimistic, and loving. Most important, students tend to feel a degree of freedom that had been previously unimaginable. This kind of dialogue tends to clarify boundaries, helping parents and adult kids feel *both* separate from each other *and* connected to each other.

Even though we have moved into adulthood, it is often the case that parts of us remain stuck in childhood in a sort of emotional time warp. The parts of us that are stuck in childhood are likely to be exemplified by certain behaviors:

- Seeking permission from our parents

- Seeking direction from our parents

- Seeking validation from our parents

- Wanting to save or rescue our parents

If these behaviors are running the show, our choices around intimate relationships will be guided by unhealed and unacknowledged stuff from the past.

Here's an example from one of my students. Trina was raised in a conservative, Southern Baptist family. Her grandmother and mother would tell her stories about girls and women from the community (ones Trina didn't know) who "went and got themselves pregnant." In a variety of ways, Trina was taught that men were not to be trusted and that sex was dangerous. She listened. At twenty-two years old, she had never gone on a date or kissed a guy, and she felt very afraid of getting close to anyone.

Before Trina interviewed her mother, she said that she couldn't see the possibility for dating or love. During the parent interview, however, Trina's mother let her know that she had had sex outside of her marriage to Trina's father. Trina was shocked! Trina's mother, too, was surprised to find out that Trina felt so ambivalent about love, and she said to her, "I hope you take a chance with love. I hope you find someone you feel really happy with, someone who cares about you."

Trina came away from the interview feeling more confused than ever. But she also came away with a sense of freedom. Rather than the absolute truth, Trina began to see her mother and grandmother's old messages to her as fear-based and extreme. Instead of a black-and-white view that "good women don't" and "bad women do," she began to see shades of gray: her mother is self-respecting, measured, and wise, *and* she explored her sexuality outside of marriage. Trina began to look at how her rigid views were on one hand keeping her safe but on the other hand keeping her stuck.

After the interview, Trina told me, "Falling in love is still somewhat frightening, but now it also feels intriguing." Notice that dialectic—*both* frightening *and* intriguing! Talking to her mother woman-to-woman gave Trina the opportunity to gather fresh data—to "grow up" her relationship with her mother. The story that Trina had been telling herself about her mother's views on love turned out to be out-of-date and inaccurate. More important, talking to her mother helped Trina realize that it is now time for Trina to make choices that suit *her* needs and *her* desires instead of someone else's. *Is it time for you to gather some fresh data of your own?*

Guidelines for Your Loving Update

If you decide to take the step of talking with your parents in the service of "growing up" your relationship with them, there are some conversation starters at the end of this lesson. You can download the "Guide to Your Loving Update" (at http://www.newharbinger.com /35814), which summarizes the entire process. Before you dive in, here's what I invite you to keep in mind:

- **Establish your boundaries** *before* **you have the conversation with your parents.** The intention of a "loving update" (Fishbane 2013) is to expand your relational self-awareness in order to help you proactively make intimate relationship choices from a place of *clarity* rather than reactively from a place of *woundedness*. The intention of this dialogue is *not* to give parents a place to confess family secrets that might end up feeling like a burden to you. Make your boundaries clear at the outset by saying something like, "I am not particularly interested in you sharing with me any secrets, especially ones about your relationship with my other parent."

- **Not all parents are available for this kind of work.** For instance, people who are active in an addiction, ensnared in an abusive relationship, or dealing with an untreated mental illness tend to be unable to connect authentically with anyone, including their adult children. Of course, there are exceptions to every rule, and I have seen parents generously try to show up for their adult child despite limitations like these.

- **You don't need to be the family therapist.** The intention of this dialogue is not to put you in the position of attempting to fix, save, or rescue your parents. This is an exercise in *being*, not *doing*. Be careful about coming away from this conversation with a to-do list (for example, "call my aunt and talk with her about my father," "send my mom some books about addiction," or "talk with my brother about how worried our parents are about him"). After the dialogue, if you are asking yourself questions like, "How can I get my mom to... ?" I invite you to view these questions as a red flag of sorts. It is most likely an indication that you are *overfunctioning*—working too hard on business that does not belong to you. Perhaps it is an old pattern for you to feel responsible for everyone's problems. If this happens, I suggest that you engage in our *Name-Connect-Choose* process. *Name* this pattern ("I notice that I am shifting into rescue mode"). *Connect* with whatever feelings are attached with the urge to fix and rescue—allowing yourself to feel sad and angry, for example—instead of reactively acting on those feelings. From that emotionally connected place, you will perhaps *choose* a different route—one that does not entangle you in your parents' problems. Instead of rescuing, you could say, "Mom, I love you very much, and I sincerely hope that you will..."

- **Avoid going into the conversation with an "ax to grind."** For example, if your father never acknowledged the eating disorder you battled as a teen, you might be hoping he will do so in this conversation. If this is the case, you will want to do two things. First, verbalize it to him: "Dad, I am aware that I am seeking validation about the bulimia I struggled with as a teen. I am not sure whether and how we will talk about that, but I want you to know that that desire is present with me today." Second, parent yourself around this, consciously validating *for yourself* what you endured. If that younger part of you feels soothed ahead of time, that part is less likely to become reactive and take over when you are with your dad. This conversation will go best if you can enter it like a reporter or an anthropologist. In other words, try to find a stance that is nonjudgmental and curious, and lead with an open heart and an open mind.

- **Explore your trepidation.** If the prospect of sitting down with your parents fills you with anxiety, it is worth understanding that feeling. As you sit with the feeling, notice where you feel it in your body. What does the nervousness feel like? What is the feeling saying? What are the thoughts that swirl around as you imagine this conversation? As you explore and honor your anxiety, it may lessen, allowing you to initiate a dialogue. Or you may decide that your anxiety is letting you know that now is not the time for a conversation like this.

- **Honor the process.** After your dialogue, you may find yourself experiencing a variety of emotions. I encourage you to allow yourself to be present with whatever feelings are stirred up within you rather than pushing them away and moving on to something else. You may cry during or after the conversation. I invite you to trust that tears have a wonderful healing quality, and your tears may also reveal new insights to you. After you talk with your parents, I encourage you to do something that makes you feel good, calm, and safe, such as taking a hot bath, walking, or journaling.

Possible Outcomes

There are many possible outcomes from this experience, but here are some common revelations that my students have shared with me over the years:

My parents are happier in their relationship than I ever thought they were. I feel relieved about this.

I feel less responsible for my parents' unhappiness. I can see how their choices led them to where they are today. I can see their problems are older than I am, and I really can feel that their problems are not mine to fix.

I am really afraid of infidelity because it happened in my family. I am still scared, but my parents shared their story with me, and at least now I understand that it didn't just happen out of the blue. It still hurts but at least it makes more sense. (Remember that in lesson 2 we talked about how stories that are more coherent and cohesive are less problematic and painful.)

There is no such thing as a perfect relationship or marriage. I knew that in my head, but talking with my parents helped me feel that more deeply. Rather than that feeling scary to me, it just feels more okay now.

For years, I have blamed my parents for problems and difficulties in my life. Talking to them adult to adult puts a little more distance between us, and I am able to feel more compassion for who they are as people. I need to be responsible for my life.

Deepening Compassion

Some people find it quite liberating to view a parent as their grandparents' child (Fishbane 2013). Viewing a parent in this way can open the door to feelings of compassion for your parent's struggles and limitations, helping you find a space beyond blame. It is important to note that holding compassion for your parent's story is not intended to excuse or condone behavior that caused you pain. Holding compassion for your parent's story is also not intended to be a bypass or a way of avoiding uncomfortable emotions like anger and sadness.

Being aware of how unhealthy patterns were transmitted from generation to generation—from your grandparents to your parent—adds thickness and context to *your* story. It provides you with a frame for your own healing and your efforts to transform old patterns so that you can love well in the here and now. And remember that this shift in perspective is available to you even if your parent is no longer alive.

Steps Toward Loving Bravely

Forging an adult-to-adult relationship with your parents is a possible, necessary, and brave step toward healthy choices in your intimate relationship.

The work in this lesson is for you to seek a "loving update" with one or more of the people who raised you.

Before

Ask your parents if they would be willing to participate in a dialogue with you, and give yourself some time to prepare. Your preparation may include visualizing how you want to think, feel, and act during the dialogue. Imagine yourself in the situation thinking, feeling, and acting in a way that feels wholehearted. Set an intention for yourself for the experience: curiosity, neutrality, connection, love, clarity, and growth are all good options.

During

Consider having a pen and paper with you during the conversation so that you can jot down information for later reflection. Or ask if you can record it. Let your parent know that it is his or her choice to answer or not answer any question that you ask. Let your parent know that either of you can ask for a break if one is wanted or needed. If you find yourself feeling emotionally overwhelmed—really angry or really sad—take a break. Find a quiet spot and take some deep breaths. You may consider having this dialogue over the course of several meetings.

Questions to Ask

Begin by asking your parent to tell you the story of his or her intimate relationship or relationships. Have your parent start by creating a verbal table of contents. Say: "Imagine your life as a story. Break the story into chapters. What would those chapters be called? What would the story of that chapter be?" As the story unfolds, you might ask follow-up questions:

What have you learned about dating?

What have you learned about marriage?

What have you learned about love?

What have you learned about handling differences and managing conflict in a relationship?

What was your marriage like when I was a kid versus today?

What do you feel are the essential ingredients in a healthy intimate relationship?

What is your life like today?

What are your passions?

What are you happy about?

What would you like me to know about you?

What do you want for me in my intimate relationship?

How do you see me as an intimate partner?

What do you think I've learned from you about being in an intimate relationship?

Information to Share

Now it's your turn to bravely share details about your present-day life:

Here's what I would like you to know about my life today…

Here's what I am struggling with…

Here's some work that I am doing on myself right now…

Here's what I want and need from you these days…

Here are some of my hopes for my future…

After

Immediately after the update, take some time for self-care. Consider taking a walk, watching TV, taking a hot bath, calling a friend, or doing whatever gives you some peaceful downtime. Then, take some time to journal about your experience, responding to these questions:

What was the high point of the dialogue for you?

What was the low point of the dialogue for you?

What was most surprising?

What does your parent see in you that you do not see (or that you see differently)?

What (if anything) about your parent's life compromised his or her ability to parent you?

Explore glimpses of compassion that you feel for your parent.

What can you see in your parent today as an adult that you could not see when you were a child?

As an adult, do you see his or her mistakes, flaws, or shortcomings in a different light than you did when you were younger?

How can thinking of your parent with compassion bring more peace to your life?

Establish Healthy Boundaries

Daring to set boundaries is about having the courage to love ourselves, even when we risk disappointing others.

—Brené Brown

Yuko and Isaac showed up for their first postwedding couples therapy session eager to share, and I was eager to listen. Amid the stories about the cake, the vows, and the honeymoon, Isaac told a story that stood out.

He said, "All day long, I was aware that my father was focusing on the things that weren't going 'right'—the rain, the photographer running late, some last-minute schedule changes. Then I bumped into him in the men's room at some point, and he said straight up, 'This is the worst wedding I have ever been to.' I put my hand on his shoulder and said, 'I'm sorry you feel that way. I'm having the time of my life.' Can you believe it? I was so proud of myself!"

Yuko chimed in, "I am so impressed with how he handled that! I could easily imagine a comment like that turning Isaac into a puddle. We've had that happen so many times before. His dad is critical, and *I'm* the one who pays the price. Suddenly, according to Isaac, everything about our life is wrong. Everything about me is wrong. It's awful when that happens. I was so relieved and delighted that he let his dad's words roll off his shoulders."

I was also delighted! Isaac had grown really tired of carrying the weight of his father's judgment, and he was beginning to choose a different path. He was clear that internalizing his father's harsh voice compromised his relationship with himself, and it compromised his relationship with Yuko. Isaac had worked hard to establish boundaries in his relationship with his father, and that hard work was paying off! Most impressive about Isaac's story was that he found a way to meet his father's remark with boundaries *and* love. He neither absorbed his father's words, letting them turn him to mush, nor pushed his father away by either retreating from him or raging at him. He felt *both* loving toward *and* separate from his father. Wow! Those are some healthy boundaries!

Where You and I Meet

Boundaries are the space between "you" and "not-you." Boundaries mark the space at which interactions occur between you and the people in your world. You can't see or touch boundaries, but they are always there.

We have a built-in sense of our *physical boundaries*, and that sense determines all kinds of behaviors, from how close we stand when we are talking to whether, when, and how we hug. We also have *emotional boundaries* that determine how much we share with others about ourselves and when. Our emotional boundaries dictate the kind of behavior we invite, tolerate, encourage, and reject from others. Being able to effectively navigate the boundary between self and other requires self-awareness and courage.

Relationships are a dance, and points of contact (boundaries) are always ripe with opportunities for flow or friction. Nothing is static. "I want more closeness." "I need some space." "That's too much." "Give me more." "Help me." "I've got this." Boundaries are anything but black-and-white. They are contextual, relational, and ever-changing. Therefore, the best we can ever hope to do in a relationship is grant each other space in which each person can state: "Hey, you're in too close." Or "Where are you? I can't feel you." Relationships in which this kind of feedback can occur are brave—and intimate—indeed!

If you can't give your partner that kind feedback—because you can't speak it or because he or she can't hear it—the relationship is guided by fear, not love. By contrast, love thrives when boundaries are consciously negotiated and renegotiated in the imperfect and dynamic flow of questions and curiosity and trying again.

I once heard an addictions specialist use a phrase that really stuck with me: *Say what you mean, mean what you say, but don't say it in a mean way.* When we are able to align what we feel on the inside with the words we speak to ourselves and to others, we can create and maintain healthy boundaries. Doing this is truly the work of a lifetime. And it is vital work. Healthy relationships require authenticity—to oneself and to another. Isaac will never be able to control how his father feels or what he says, but Isaac does have control over his reactions to his father's words. His commitment to creating a boundary by speaking his truth in the face of his father's judgment helps him—and it helps his marriage.

Although several forthcoming lessons will invite you to look at how you manage boundaries in romantic relationships, we will focus first on boundaries between you and members of your family, because it can be easy to underestimate the impact that family boundaries have on your love life. This is true for people who are single, dating, or married. A review of this material is available online at http://www.newharbinger.com/35814.

Energy In, Energy Out

We know that a boundary is the point of contact between two people, so imagine that when two people are together, energy is flowing within each of them and also between the two of them. When boundaries are healthy, you maintain the energy that is yours and your partner maintains the energy that is his or hers. Both of you are able to feel *connected to* each other and *separate from* each other. Boundaries are unhealthy when they are too porous or too rigid.

Let's break these unhealthy boundaries down:

	Input	**Output**
Healthy Boundary (Connected and Protected)	We connect with others while holding on to ourselves.	We express our opinions and perspectives while respecting the views and voices of others.
Porous Boundary (Connected but not Protected)	We absorb or take on that which is not ours.	We intrude into that which is not ours.
Rigid Boundary (Protected but not Connected)	We block the input of others.	We restrain or hold ourselves back from others.

Porous Boundaries

Porous boundaries mean that we are *connected* but not *protected*. Perhaps we are too wide open to the input of others, losing ourselves in efforts to please and placate. Or, we are meddling in stuff that isn't our business.

Absorbing

Are there relational moments in which you feel *overly responsible*—to fix, to heal, to compensate for? When you take on that which is not yours, you allow yourself to be drained, with others taking what you have not lovingly given. If Isaac had absorbed his father's comment, it would likely have altered his entire wedding day, leading him to scramble to try to please him. His wedding day story would have been about how his dad ruined everything, and he would have become the victim of his father's judgment. Instead Isaac managed his boundary. He did not absorb his father's comment, refusing to take on something that he knew was not his. His father's words were a reflection of *his father's story*, which was ultimately neither Isaac's business nor his concern. This whole notion that we do not need to take on another person's story as our own is not *easy*, but it is *simple*.

Intruding

Do you *intrude* into spaces where you are not wanted or needed—inserting yourself, ignoring feedback, demanding what hasn't been given in love? For me, I know that I'm violating the boundaries of someone else when I catch myself saying or thinking, "But I'm just trying to help." When invited, being of service to someone at a time of need can be powerfully compassionate and intimate, but sometimes we just slip into someone else's business. Sometimes as an escape or a distraction from our own business! One of my dear friends says, "How full of me to be so full of you!"

I can imagine Yuko facing this risk in the aftermath of her father-in-law's comment. If she begins to act on Isaac's behalf, confronting his father or insisting that Isaac keep his distance from him, she's exiting her own business and taking residence in Isaac's. "I'm just trying to help" usually comes from a loving place. Perhaps Isaac *will* enlist her help or feel grateful if she offers, but any intervention must be guided by a conversation between Isaac and Yuko. Connecting with someone's pain while staying in your own business is hard to do! It is difficult to see people we care about in pain, but don't underestimate the power of bearing witness, without agenda, to the pain of another. When we bear witness without trying to fix, we create connection while practicing healthy boundaries.

Rigid Boundaries

Rigid boundaries mean that we are *protected* but not *connected*. Perhaps we are cut off from the input of others, refusing to be influenced or swayed. Or maybe we are shut down and struggling to open ourselves or express what is inside us.

Blocking

In some of your relationships, do you feel vigilant, on guard, and afraid of being ambushed? When our boundaries are rigid, we may find ourselves refusing to let in the input of others, usually for fear of being attacked. We feel brittle, edgy, and defensive...and we probably come across that way too. If Isaac's boundaries had been rigid in that moment with his father, he likely would have fought back, expressing some version of, "Screw you, Dad!" In this stance, instead of trusting ourselves to let in, "metabolize," and let go of other people's energy, we block everything.

Restraining

If those around you say you feel hard to reach or complain that you don't open up, it might be that you rigidly hold yourself back from self-expression. Perhaps you keep a tight rein on self-expression because you learned early on that it wasn't safe to give voice to your feelings. Sometimes we get stuck holding tightly to an old way of coping, long after it has served its original purpose. Healthy relational boundaries mean letting others know how their words or actions make us feel. Restraining ourselves from sharing our internal world with other people can leave us feeling resentful and devitalized.

Fences

Committing to an intimate relationship involves creating a *we*. In order to become a member of that we, each partner has to transform his or her relationship with the family he or she grew up in. As we know from earlier lessons in this book, the goal is to feel *both* separate from *and* connected to our family of origin. This process of becoming separate from while staying connected to is called *differentiation*, and it tends to happen over time.

If you remain too wrapped up in the family you came from, your partner will feel that your loyalty has not transferred over to the new family you are creating together. But at the other extreme, if you are too cut off from the people who raised you, your intimate relationship may feel isolated and disconnected from your community, your heritage, your lineage. Being in love can help you feel more *differentiated* from your family of origin, as you begin to create your own couple-specific traditions and rituals. It is also the case that in order to be in love, you need to be at least somewhat differentiated from the family you grew up in. Otherwise, family needs and expectations will prevent the intimate relationship from getting off the ground.

So what would be just about right? My friend and mentor (and foreword writer) Dr. Mona Fishbane uses the metaphor of a picket fence to capture the boundary that is needed between adult kids and their parents (2013). Each generation is on its own side of the fence, yet they can see and feel each other. Connection is possible, but what happens on one side of the fence doesn't need to be the other person's business. The picket-fence image captures the heart of differentiation—we are separate from each other but we are also connected to each other. We can enjoy each other's company while enjoying our boundaries as well.

Culture

This all sounds perfectly nice in theory, but, in the real world, couples spend a lot of time and energy figuring out (and fighting about) how to navigate boundaries. That's because in between the extremes of total separateness and total connection are many shades of gray, and what feels to me like just the right mix might feel awful to you. How we manage our boundaries is profoundly impacted by culture.

Cultural factors like race, ethnicity, religion, and geographic region shape how we interact with each other. Culture dictates (implicitly and explicitly) what's "normal," "healthy," and "acceptable." What might look extreme in one culture may be common and not problematic in another culture. For example, research indicates that Greek and Italian couples touch each other more when they are interacting than do English, French, and Dutch couples (Lyubomirsky 2013). A colleague of mine used to say that the closer you get to the equator, the more the weather heats up *and* the more the people "heat up" in terms of personality, emotionality, and desire for closeness. Sweeping generalization? Yes. Some truth? Yes. Culture dictates how we "do" boundaries.

When two people come together across cultural differences, relational self-awareness is their best guide to figuring out how to handle the bridging of different worlds. Imagine, for example, that a Caucasian American woman has dinner for the first time with her Chinese American boyfriend's family. To her, the atmosphere feels uncomfortably formal, and she is struck by how much deference her boyfriend shows to his parents. The boundaries feel way too rigid to her. On the flip side, when he is with her family, he feels uncomfortable with the casual atmosphere, which he interprets as disrespectful. The boundaries feel too porous to him. His desire to please and accommodate his parents feels dutiful to him, but she feels abandoned by what she perceives as him putting them before her. Her playful approach with her parents feels like an expression of love to her, but he feels like an outsider.

Without relational self-awareness, they are likely to turn these cultural differences into judgments, each labeling their own family's way to be the better way and the other family's way to be the worse way. With relational self-awareness, they can name their reactions. He can say, "When I am with your family, here's how I start to feel…" From a place of curiosity instead of judgment, they can together weave a story of how their love is big enough and strong enough to hold these cultural differences.

Boundaries in Action

Maria is thirty-two years old and actively dating. She and her mother are very close, so her pattern has been to go on a date and then call her mom to "debrief." Her mother has lots of opinions and is not afraid to express them: "An accountant? Boring!" "Shorter than you? Are you serious?!" "Split the bill? Come on!" In Maria's gut, she feels troubled by this, knowing the boundary between them is too porous. She's absorbing too much. Her mom's voice plays inside her head, shaping her experience of these men. However, she feels afraid to speak up, worried that her mom will feel offended and hurt.

Knowing that it's time to make a change, she first allows herself to *name* this pattern ("In my family, asking for a firmer boundary feels like a betrayal"). She allows herself to *connect* with all the feelings she has about this old story. Maria feels sad that it's so hard for her to stand up for herself, and she feels angry that it's so hard for her mother to trust that Maria can love her and also need some distance from her. She decides it's time to *choose* something new and plans to keep the details of her dates to herself, at least until she is able to hear her own voice loud and clear. Now, if her mother asks about a recent date, Maria simply says, "Thank you for asking. I don't really have anything to share right now." That's an example of *say what you mean, mean what you say, but don't say it in a mean way.*

After trying that a few times, Maria decides to let her mother know about the insight she has had and the new choice she is making. She tells her, "Mom, I have become aware that when I share details about my first dates, I find myself really swayed by your opinions and perspective. It makes it harder for me to discern my own feelings about this new relationship. I appreciate your interest, but I am going to hold back from talking about my dating life with you for a while and see how that feels for me." Renegotiating this boundary led to a gentler and more compassionate dialogue between Maria and her mother in a few other arenas as well. Maria feels more able to vulnerably share stories from her world, knowing that she can trust herself to advocate on her own behalf if needed.

As Gandhi said, "Happiness is when what you think, what you say, and what you do are in harmony." Learning to create and maintain healthy boundaries is the work of a lifetime. The payoff is so worthwhile: relationships that invite and demand authenticity and integrity.

Steps Toward Loving Bravely

Intimate relationships are shaped by the past as well as by the here-and-now relationship that you have with the people who raised you. Healthy boundaries honor both autonomy and connection, allowing you to enjoy your intimate relationship without guilt, fear, or shame.

Boundary Matters

Complete the table below to help you reflect on how you tend to manage boundaries in your relationships. You can also find this table online at http://www.newharbinger.com/35814.

Type of Boundary	With whom do you have this type of boundary?	Example of this boundary in action
Healthy boundary		
Absorbing (Porous Input Boundary)		
Intruding (Porous Output Boundary)		
Blocking (Rigid Input Boundary)		
Restraining (Rigid Output Boundary)		

Analyze the Data

In order to better understand how you manage relational boundaries, answer the following questions about your "Boundary Matters" table:

> What patterns did you notice as you completed the table? Do your boundaries tend to be healthier in some relationships than others (friends versus family versus intimate relationships)?

> Is there one kind of unhealthy boundary that you seem to tend toward?

Reflect on a specific example of an unhealthy relationship boundary from your "Boundary Matters" table.

> Write a little about the specific incident that captures the unhealthy nature of that boundary. What happened before, during, and after?

> What made it difficult for you to manage a healthy boundary in that situation (for example, fear of hurting the other person's feelings, anxiety, feeling powerless)?

> At what point did you realize the boundary was unhealthy? What helped you see that?

> Does this incident remind you of patterns in your family of origin? In what way?

> Looking back on this incident, what do you wish you would have done differently?

> If this situation happens again in the future, how do you want to handle it?

Love and Family

Think about whether differences in family boundaries have been a problem in your intimate relationships. For example, "My family talks on the phone once a month; her family talks on the phone every day." Answer the following questions:

To what extent have you found yourself judging the relationship that your intimate partner has with his or her family, especially in terms of boundary management?

What is it specifically that triggers or upsets you about this dynamic?

What do you come to believe about your partner when confronted with this kind of difference in your intimate relationship? About yourself?

Journal about what would need to shift within you so that you could view this as a *difference* between your families versus "my family is good, right, and normal, and your family is bad, wrong, and abnormal."

PART 2

Self-Awareness

Lesson 6

Embrace Your Unique Love Truths

A human being is a part of the whole called by us universe, a part limited in time and space.

—Albert Einstein

As Spanish philosopher José Ortega y Gasset said: "I am I plus my circumstances." In earlier lessons, we explored the "circumstances" of our family stories about love, but it is also the case that the circumstances of our *zeitgeist*—the place and time in which we live—also shape how we feel about ourselves and our intimate relationships. For example, an unmarried twenty-five-year-old woman in the United States in the 1920s would likely have been in a full-blown panic (or at least her parents would have been) about her marital status. Today, it is normal to be twenty-five and single.

Our culture sends us messages about who and when and how to love—messages that shape how we feel within our skin, how we make choices about intimate relationships, and how we feel about those choices. Many of us are blindly guided by sweeping cultural "shoulds." But when we are able to *name* how cultural messages and stories live within, we open up new possibilities for how we feel and how we relate to our intimate partners. When we are able to discern where and when and how cultural stories mesh with our own deep truth, we put ourselves in charge of our love life. But that's easier said than done because *our culture is the air we breathe* day in and day out, seeping into our pores without us even noticing. The goal isn't to escape our cultural context. Because consciousness facilitates choice, the goal instead is to decide whether a particular cultural message limits us or supports us. Nowhere are these external voices louder than around our shared cultural stories about *autonomy versus connection* and about *gender norms.*

"I" and "We"

The desire to love and be loved is woven into our DNA. Connection is our default setting. But it's not quite that simple, is it? In addition to connection, most of us crave solitude, independence, and freedom. When the desire for connection competes with the desire for autonomy, we can end up feeling lost and anxious, asking questions like:

How do I balance wanting to be in a relationship with wanting to have "my own life?"

Why do I want to be in a relationship only until I am in one— and then I can only think of what I'm missing out on?

How do I blend my life with someone else's without losing myself?

There's no doubt that navigating these seemingly opposing forces—the desire for connection and the desire for autonomy—is easier when we trust what is inside of us. In order to trust what is within, we need to first *name* the external messages that we take in about how connected or autonomous we "should" be. Then, we need to *connect* with the impact that those messages have on us. It is only when we have identified these external messages and figured out how we feel about them that we are freed up to *choose* a path that make us feel good, authentic, and whole.

American culture prizes independence. Sociologists classify cultures on a spectrum from valuing the individual (individualistic) to valuing the community (collectivistic), and the United States falls squarely on the individualistic end of that spectrum. In contrast,

Asian, South American, and African countries tend to fall more toward the collectivistic end of the spectrum. A student of mine who spent her early years in a collectivistic culture and immigrated to the United States as a teen explained to me that when she thinks of her "self," she thinks of her family. Her sense of self is inextricably and deeply bound to her family unit. When faced with decisions, she thinks primarily of the impact of her choices on her family and is guided by that.

Of course, people born and raised in the United States factor in others and feel a sense of loyalty to family, but we value standing on our own two feet and being our own person. This makes perfect sense since the United States was formed in order to escape the control and domination of England. Life, *liberty*, and the pursuit of happiness. It's right there! We prize freedom and the ability to chart our own course. Do I believe that the words of the US Constitution play in our heads as we are falling in love? No. Do I believe that growing up in an individualistic culture affects our choices in our intimate relationship? Yes.

Clients and students often express worry that falling in love means risking "losing myself"—a concern that makes sense in the context of an individualistic culture. Valuing individualism can make us feel squeamish about the fact that falling in love means becoming dependent on another person—emotionally, pragmatically, and financially. The dependence, or really, *interdependence*, goes in both directions. Love requires the cocreation of a *we*—something bigger than the two individuals. The *we* has needs different from the needs of either individual. The *we* must be nurtured and tended. And the *we* provides benefits: comfort, a home base, and shared resources.

Doing Gender

If we want to bravely and humbly honor *both* the need for closeness *and* the need for independence, we must peek through the gender lens. Traditionally, we talk about women as sitting on the *commitment-craving* end of the spectrum and men hanging out on the *commitment-phobic* end of the spectrum. While this is certainly a sweeping generalization, it does reflect our cultural stories about masculinity and femininity. This concept could be an entire book unto itself, so I will just offer a simple (and silly) example of how we "load" masculinity with independence/autonomy and we "load" femininity with dependence/connection. Walk the aisles of your local costume store in October, and you are sure to find a bride costume designed for a girl to wear. But I would bet you any amount of money that you will not find a groom costume designed for a boy to wear.

From the first days of their lives, boys are flooded with stories that encourage them (more like force them) to be independent, to stand on their own two feet. "Don't cry." "Man up." "Don't back down." Think about the words that are used to shame a boy or a man for showing vulnerability, dependence, or need: "sissy" and "girly" (there are more graphic ones, but I'll leave it there…). These gender-loaded words encourage hypermasculinity and degrade that which is associated with femininity: softness, connection, dependence.

Times are changing. Our continued efforts to embrace people whose sexualities and gender identities have been marginalized and oppressed serve all of us. The degree to which each of us can embrace all of the manifestations of what we call masculine and feminine is the degree to which we can live with increasing authenticity and integrity. Strict gender binaries relegate us to being "half-humans." In fact, the mere act of labeling desires, thoughts, and behaviors as being either "masculine" or "feminine" puts us into boxes that just don't fit. We need and deserve access to the full spectrum of human experience.

We all yearn for power and control. We all have the potential to be aggressive and violent. We all have longings to nurture and care for others. We all crave intimacy and closeness. *These are all part of the human experience.* And…there's nothing like an intimate relationship to bring each and every one of these longings out in full force! In order to create a sustaining and happy intimate partnership, you *must* be able to embrace all of your so-called "masculine" energy and your so-called "feminine" energy. And you also must be willing to tolerate, accept, and embrace the same in your partner. When you find yourself falling back on a cultural gender story, be willing to look inside and ask yourself what is getting *triggered*—stirred up—in you. Do any of these prompts sound familiar?

"A real man doesn't…"

"What kind of wife…"

"As a man, you should…"

"Women are so…"

It's helpful to view that language as a little red flag and then ask yourself:

What do I feel in my body?

What is upsetting me right now? What am I afraid of?

What am I desiring right now?

Whose gender story is this? To what degree is it serving me and my relationship right now? To what degree is it constraining or limiting me and my relationship right now?

We are most at risk of using a narrow gender (ex. As a man, you should…) story when we feel scared, alone, and/or hurt in a relationship. It is usually an effort to make the other person behave differently so that we can feel better (less anxious, less vulnerable, more in control). Connection deepens when partners commit to finding, again and again, a space beyond simple, thin, and ill-fitting stories about who people should be based on the bodies they occupy.

Self-awareness about gender stories is as important for people in the LGBTQ (lesbian, gay, bisexual, transgender, and queer) community as it is for those who identify as heterosexual. Each of us has a relationship to masculinity and femininity, because our culture is gendered. In order to love deeply and bravely, we need to be (and deserve to be) conscious of our gender stories regardless of whether we look, feel, identify, and behave in ways that are masculine, feminine, both, or neither.

Playing with Energy

I took us right to the dark side of cultural gender stories—how we use ideas about what masculinity and femininity "should be" to protect ourselves when we feel unsafe and unsettled in our intimate relationships. But cultural gender stories can elevate and connect us, too. Taking pride in how you manifest your masculinity or femininity can be a potent source of self-esteem (for example, feeling sexy in a dress that accentuates your curves or feeling more handsome with a beard). Elements of masculinity and femininity shape the attraction between partners (for example, being drawn in by those curves or that facial hair).

Willingness to look at the subtle and not-so-subtle ways that masculinity and femininity show up in your relationship opens the door to freedom and flexibility. Use masculinity and femininity where and when it serves connection to self and connection to other. Find a space *beyond* masculinity and femininity when gender stories are putting you or your partner in a box. A heterosexual female student shared that she loves holding her boyfriend (being the big spoon)...until she panics that it means she's too "manly" and he's too "girly." When she shared this, I felt sad. An abstract cultural gender story had become a little prison, keeping her from enjoying what felt natural and intuitive to her.

This whole topic of gender stories and love hits close to home for me. In fact, my husband, Todd, and I never would have become a couple if I hadn't taken Introduction to Women's Studies during my sophomore year at the University of Michigan. Backstory: Todd and I lived across the hall from each other in our freshman year. We quickly became close friends—I was drawn to his sense of humor, generosity, and gentleness. I loved how "me" I felt when I was with him. No pretense. Lots of authenticity. It became clear that his feelings for me were going from "friends" to "more than friends," but I was holding myself back. The package he came in didn't fit with my very narrow definition of masculinity. He was shorter than me (and still is). He didn't own any tools (and still doesn't). He didn't enjoy fishing or hunting (and still doesn't). I didn't know how to get past that, so I kept him in a "friend box" in my head. Until I took a Women's Studies class in which I learned that our culture heaps a dizzying number of assumptions and "shoulds" onto a male body and a female body. It was as if someone opened a door for me!

Suddenly, rather than feeling fearful that I couldn't be drawn to him because he didn't manifest masculine qualities in the way that felt familiar to me (read: how *my dad* and *step-dad* manifest masculine qualities), I had the freedom to get in touch with all the ways that I did (and do) feel drawn to him: his smell, his hairy chest, his touch, his even temper, his ability to solve problems—a different kind of handyman. Becoming aware of how I had internalized cultural gender stories set him free from the tiny prison *inside my mind*. It also set me free! I could be the one with the toolbox, and I could be nearly six feet tall without apology. Awareness of the sneaky ways that gender stories infiltrate our intimate relationships grants us the space to choose, consciously, what works and what doesn't work for us—rather than automatically going with what society dictates we "should" do.

We will never transcend our cultural context, but our self-awareness is our trusted guide as we figure out how to live well among a bombardment of noisy and often-conflicting messages about love. "Be your own person!" "Let someone love you!" "Don't back down!" "Lean in!" Being able to look critically at our culture's stories (especially about dependence and gender) is a gateway to freedom. The happiest couples I know are the ones who are able to create and inhabit love stories that are good enough. Not perfect: good enough.

Steps Toward Loving Bravely

As we name cultural stories and connect with how those stories shape us, we can choose a path that honors our unique love truths.

Leaning on Each Other

Take a look at the list of words and phrases below, and circle the ones that you heard or still hear most often in the family you grew up in:

Alone	Together	Sacrifice	Mine
Ours	We	Me	You
Us	I	Unit	Independent
Myself	Family	They	Our culture
Our values	Our beliefs	Tradition	Ritual
Individual	Duty	Loyalty	Obligation
Selfish	Selfless	Separate	Commitment

Take a look at the words you circled, and decide where your family falls on a continuum from *individualistic* (operating as individuals living under the same roof) to *collectivistic* (operating as a unit).

Individualistic ——————————————— **Collectivistic**

Next, think about whether your family's "we-ness" shapes your family's story about *interdependence*. In what ways did the people in your family of origin give the message "You can lean on us" versus "Stand on your own two feet"? On the next page, mark with an X the place on this spectrum your family falls.

Independent ——————— Interdependent ——————— Dependent
(Stand on your   (We lean on   (Don't leave us)
own two feet)   each other)

Now return to the words above. Circle the three words that best capture what *you* value most in an intimate relationship. Are these words similar to or different from the words you circled about your family of origin? What is your reaction to this?

Finally, return to the spectrum from independent to dependent and circle the place on the spectrum where you would like your intimate relationship to fall. Notice where the circle is relative to where the X is. What is your reaction to this?

Sharing Your Gender Story

Meet up with a friend, family member, or partner and take turns sharing your gender stories using the following questions as your guide:

What were early messages you got about being a boy or being a girl?

What did you come to believe about what people of your sex should or shouldn't do?

What activities, toys, opportunities, et cetera did you not take advantage of because of your sex?

In what ways did the messages you received about your gender help your self-confidence? Hurt your self-confidence?

What feelings come up in you as you share your gender story?

When one of you is being the storyteller, make sure the other person is practicing *mindful listening* by doing the following:

- Listen in order to understand, not in order to respond. Keep your attention in the present moment. If you find your mind wandering or thinking about your own answers

to these questions, bring your attention back to simply
listening.

- Make only reflective and validating comments: "I see"
  or "wow."

- Ask only clarifying questions: "Can you tell me more
  about that?" "What do you mean by that?"

- Avoid giving advice or attempting to influence the other
  person's perspective.

After each of you has had the opportunity to share your gender
story and to listen mindfully, talk together about the following:

What were some similarities and differences in your stories?

What felt surprising or upsetting to each of you about this
exercise?

What was it like to listen mindfully? To what degree was it
similar to how you usually listen? To what degree was it a new
experience for you?

What was it like to be mindfully listened to? To what degree
was *that* a new experience for you?

Lesson 7

Surrender the Fairy Tale

Commitment is inherent in any genuinely loving relationship.

—M. Scott Peck

All fairy tales seem to end the same way, don't they? "And they lived happily ever after." Romantic comedies too…the couple walks hand in hand into the sunset, more or less. We never get the chance to fast-forward and see the couple on an ordinary Tuesday evening, paying bills and watching Netflix. The images of love that we consume through television and movies tend to be highly romanticized and idealized, quite far removed from the realities and complexities of a real intimate relationship. What impact does that have on us?

For my dissertation research, I interviewed heterosexual couples who had been married for between one and three years, asking them to tell me their "love stories" (Solomon 2001). One of the questions I would ask toward the end was "How would you say that married life, in reality, compares to your expectations of how it would be?" I was surprised by how many of them told me that the realities of married life felt disappointing. One woman said, "I just thought we'd look at each other differently. Or there would be this feeling when we were sitting on the couch watching TV, but nope, we're sitting on the couch watching TV." Another expressed, "I just thought it was going to be more like talking about things, talking about our feelings…and that doesn't happen."

Real-life love stories don't look the way they do on our screens, and real-life love stories change over time. In this lesson, we will explore how real love, in real relationships, changes and evolves—and how *we must* change and evolve as well.

Love Stories Also Have Chapters

Every intimate relationship is a love story with unique chapters that detail a couple's highs, lows, special events, and turning points, yet in most love stories, three major chapters almost always make an appearance:

Early Idealization → *The Fall from Grace* → *Brave Love*

When two people meet and begin to fall in love, the first chapter, *Early Idealization,* predominates. What stands out to you most are those qualities that you feel make your partner extraordinary. He is the funniest, the smartest, and the sexiest. Research has indicated, in fact, that the brain of someone who is falling in love resembles the brain of someone who is addicted to drugs or struggling with obsessive-compulsive disorder (Fisher 2004; Parker-Pope 2007). As we fall in love, we tend to be obsessive, yearning, craving, and prone to ruminative thinking about our beloved. This state of affairs cannot go on forever. People have to work, after all! Idealization is an untenable biochemical stew inside of your brain. Plus, humans are far too fallible for this kind of relationship. At some point, the funniest-smartest-sexiest man you've ever met will inevitably do something un-funny, un-smart, or un-sexy, calling your idealization into question.

When he falls from his pedestal, chapter 1 ends and chapter 2 begins: *The Fall from Grace.* He forgets to call when he says he will. He says something insensitive. It might be you who falls from your pedestal first, freaking out the morning of a big presentation and shattering his image of you as calm, cool, and collected. The fall from grace may come in the form of your first fight or the first time you face a crisis together (such as the loss of a job, a health scare, or a family member's death). Regardless of the triggering event, the fall from grace will come. Even though it is normal and inevitable, the shift it creates in a relationship can feel quite upsetting, disappointing, and confusing.

All hope is not lost. Because when couples survive the fall from grace, they end up in a pretty amazing chapter: *Brave Love*. Brave love is an authentic and deeply connected place in which both partners get to be imperfect *and* worthy of love. As happy couples describe, "I can just be myself." People in this love chapter have a different brain chemistry from people in the early stages of love. The relationship is now fueled by the chemicals of *attachment*—oxytocin and vasopressin (Fisher 2004). When we are attached to each other, we value feeling safe, trusted, and trusting. In that place of brave love, both partners are committed to a "relationship of constancy," as M. Scott Peck calls it, showing up again and again for the relationship because it feels worthwhile and because you promised you would. People in this chapter of love enjoy the benefits of security but may also struggle to maintain a passionate connection.

Here's how moving through these chapters looks in real life. My client Diana was married at the time, but it didn't keep her from falling hard and fast for Tom. Ten years older, Tom was a handsome, successful, and well-known businessman. She was deeply unhappy in her marriage, and Tom represented everything her husband was not. She left her marriage and lapped up every ounce of Early Idealization. Tom was certainly easy for her to idealize…until he was staying at her place and got hit with a raging case of food poisoning. Seeing him weak, needy, and quite literally out of control rattled her deeply. She came to our next therapy session questioning him, questioning herself, and questioning the whole relationship. "This is what I left my marriage for?" she said. I wondered out loud to her whether their love story had just been flung headfirst out of the romance of Early Idealization into the messiness of the Fall from Grace. Framing it this way—as an inevitable and normal development—gave her comfort and allowed us to explore what, exactly, from her individual life story led her to feel so triggered by their fall from grace.

See whether any of the following statements sound familiar to you:

> It's hard to let myself fall for someone. I protect myself from how scary and vulnerable it is to like someone that much by being critical and really picky of him or her.

> It's hard to let someone fall for me. I am uncomfortable up on that pedestal. I wonder what's wrong with the person if he or she is so into me.

> I freak out during the Fall from Grace chapter. I tend to leave at the first sign of a problem.

> I feel able to handle the first fight, but I keep partnering with people who don't want to get down in the muck with me.

> That Brave Love chapter is hard for me. I start feeling bored and disappointed. I crave novelty.

> To me, Brave Love feels too "normal." I don't trust it.

It is possible to struggle in any or all of these chapters, and there are no easy or obvious fixes. Know that it is brave to even *look* at your patterns and tendencies, and identifying a tender spot within you puts you miles ahead of those whose story is a flat, thin "I just haven't found the right person yet."

If you have identified a chapter in which you tend to struggle, here are some ideas to keep in mind:

- **Name it to tame it.** The mere act of identifying (naming) a pattern or tendency changes your relationship to the pattern or tendency (Siegel 2010).

- **Become aware and make a choice.** When a pattern is brought out into the open, into your conscious awareness, you have choices including talking about your pattern with your intimate partner. There is a back-and-forth dynamic between trust and intimacy: intimacy grows trust, and trust paves the way for deeper intimacy.

- **Tie the present to the past.** How does this particular pattern relate to an old story that you carry from the family you grew up in?

- **Embrace the both/and.** Look for a dialectic that may be hidden within your feelings. For example: "I am *both* afraid of conflict *and* trusting of myself to handle it."

Remember that we come by our relationship "stuff" for good reasons. Taking note of where fear rears its head in your intimate relationship gives you an opportunity to go deep and expand your relational self-awareness.

Should I Stay or Should I Go?

Although there are lessons to be learned in every intimate relationship, not every relationship can or should make it to the Brave Love chapter. Relationships end. Students and therapy clients frequently ask themselves (and me), "How do I know whether to stay or go?" Ending an intimate relationship is deeply personal, so it is impossible to speak in absolutes. However, it is worthwhile to identify some relationship dynamics that signal that you're experiencing something more than a fall from grace—you're experiencing a relationship with a poor prognosis.

Untreated Addiction

Untreated addiction to alcohol, drugs, gambling, pornography, and so on in one or both partners wreaks havoc on an intimate relationship. I am careful to say *untreated* addiction. People who are practicing their recovery often create incredibly rich intimate relationships because they have stripped away defenses, come face-to-face with their wounds and fears, and lived to tell about it.

Unfortunately, no intimate relationship can compete with an active addiction. Addiction is just too powerful.

Abuse

Abuse (emotional, sexual, or physical) and love cannot exist in the same space at the same time. As feminist scholar Dr. bell hooks says, "Abuse and neglect negate love. Care and affirmation, the opposite of abuse and humiliation, are the foundation of love. No one can rightfully claim to be loving when behaving abusively" (2000, 22). When there is abuse in an intimate relationship, individual therapy is needed for both partners. The one who is being abusive must explore and heal whatever is triggering the abusive behavior—usually having been a victim of abuse as a child. And the one who is being abused must have space and time to heal, reestablishing boundaries, self-love, and self-worth.

Patterns of Dishonesty and Betrayal

Infidelity is a relationship-changer. In the wake of an affair, some couples choose to stay together and rebuild—hard work that in the best-case scenario grows both partners. Other couples end their relationship. The prognosis is worse when infidelity is a recurring problem, indicating a pattern of deceit. Remember that dishonesty and betrayal take other forms, too, such as lying about money and work.

Lack of Love

Research shows that couples therapists rank a lack of love to be the most difficult problem to treat—more difficult even than addiction or infidelity (Whisman, Dixon, and Johnson 1997). We value love as the glue that holds an intimate relationship together. In fact, the vast majority of Americans (93 percent) report that love is the most important factor in marrying someone (Pew Research Center

2010). When we say, "I love you, but I'm not 'in love' with you," it may mean that we need to ask ourselves: "What is keeping me from showing up fully and engaging in this relationship? Where is my passion, enthusiasm, and engagement if not here in the relationship?"

As we discussed earlier in this lesson, keeping passion alive is the long-term work of love, and it is the work of both partners. However, a lack of love is different. It usually indicates that a relationship was built initially for pragmatic or strategic reasons (for example, an unplanned pregnancy). Sometimes love grows from nothing (many arranged marriages begin with a commitment and become rich love stories), but sometimes it does not.

Asymmetrical Revitalization

Last, I want to touch on a subtle but troubling dynamic that Thomas Moore (1995) calls "asymmetrical revitalization." This term captures a situation in which one partner is invested in being self-reflective, open, and curious about the rich and mysterious world of the intimate relationship, and the other partner is not. Jacob and Wendy are a couple like this. Jacob views conflict as an opportunity to learn more about how each of them perceives the world, the self, and each other. He is curious about what makes him tick, and he values relationship talk. Wendy prefers to sweep stuff under the rug as quickly as possible. As she says, "I don't do feelings." He implored her to do couples therapy with him because he felt they were drifting apart. She refused. After years of feeling that he lacked a partner in the deepest sense, he ended the relationship. Asymmetrical revitalization challenges a relationship because it leaves partners feeling that they are on different wavelengths.

A Brave Love Fairy Tale

When I hear people say, "I don't believe in couples therapy," it is a red flag to me. I stifle the urge to say, "Couples therapy is not Santa Claus. It exists!" Not believing in couples therapy is rooted in a fairy tale full of abstract *shoulds*: Love should be easy; we should be able to handle this on our own; people should keep their problems to themselves. Taking a stand against couples therapy is like drowning but refusing to reach for the life preserver that is being offered. In the "Marriage 101" course, I implore students to say yes if and when their intimate partner asks, "Can we do some couples therapy?" And I implore you to say yes as soon as you are asked, even if you don't really love the idea. When couples therapy begins after months or years of stalling and avoiding, a large wall of negativity has been built. Couples therapy is challenging as it is. Why make it harder by having to do the difficult work of tearing down, brick by brick, a wall of resentment built because it took so long to get help?

If we peered into the ordinary Tuesday evening of our favorite fairy-tale couple, living out their happily ever after, I hope we would see them embodying *brave love*—respecting romance yet tolerating disappointment, inviting passion yet navigating frustration, seeking deep connection yet enduring conflict. Identifying yourself as a "hopeless romantic" is totally fine, as long as your fairy tale includes dark days and courage in the face of challenges.

Steps Toward Loving Bravely

Intimate relationships involve messy, confusing, beautiful work that makes you grow and evolve like nothing else can. Surrender the fairy tale and embrace brave love.

I Am Grateful

Living in a space of brave love requires staying present to all the ways that goodness permeates your life, as it is right here and right now. Therefore, if you don't already, begin to keep a gratitude journal. This simple practice can shift your perspective toward seeing what is good, right, and plentiful in your world, releasing fear, craving, and envy. It is one of the easiest and most effective self-care practices around, and research has indicated that practices that increase feelings of gratitude are correlated with happier relationships, better emotional health, and less stress (Wood, Froh, and Geraghty 2010; Gordon, Arnette, and Smith 2011). You can keep a notebook next to your bed or you can download a gratitude journal app like the one at http://www.getgratitude.co. Some people like to spend a few minutes at the end of each day writing down a few things they are grateful for. Others prefer one longer weekly entry.

Here are a few tips for keeping a gratitude journal:

- Instead of just mindlessly going through the motions, take a moment and say to yourself that you are doing this for your well-being and to improve the quality of your relationship.

- Focus on people, not just things.

- Focus on what is surprising or unexpected.

- Reflect on what your life would be like without those blessings.

Love Chapters

Write a table of contents for one of your intimate relationships, past or current, making sure that you name each chapter. Then reflect on the extent to which the love-story chapters we talked about in this lesson—Early Idealization, The Fall from Grace, Brave Love—fit your love story. How have you handled the opportunities and challenges of each of these chapters?

If you have had more than one significant intimate relationship, you might want to create a table of contents for each and then compare them to each other. What patterns stand out to you?

Keep the Soul in Soulmate

A soulmate is the one person whose love is powerful enough to motivate you to meet your soul, to do the emotional work of self-discovery, of awakening.

—Kenny Loggins

What do you collect? Whether it be action figures, books, or antique porcelain frogs, I'm guessing there's something you enjoy gathering and treasuring. For me, it's beach glass and quotes about love, especially quotes about *soulmates*, and the Kenny Loggins quote is just one of many in my collection. The theme of soulmates is one of my favorite love-related topics to explore because it invites multiple perspectives, and the topic creates the opportunity to ask, "What do I believe?"

First things first: Here's what I *don't* believe. I don't believe that your soulmate is your perfect match. Research by social psychologists Spike W. S. Lee and Norbert Schwartz (2014) indicates that believing your soulmate is your perfect match can set you up for unhealthy patterns. They found that people who use a perfect-match definition of soulmates tend to experience overreactions to conflict and lower relationship satisfaction. It makes sense, right? If I believe that you are my perfect match, when we bump up against inevitable conflict or our "fall from grace," I am going to feel disappointed and confused. People who subscribe to this perspective tend to use the language of *should* when talking about love: "It shouldn't feel like this." "We shouldn't have this problem."

Soulmates Three Ways

Awareness of your stance on the notion of soulmates is more than a philosophical exercise. *How you relate to the soulmate idea impacts how you think, feel, and act in your intimate relationship.* In the service of relational self-awareness, let's journey through three perspectives on soulmates. I'll weigh in on each as we go (no surprise!). Before you read the three perspectives below, write down any current beliefs you have about soulmates, and see whether your perspective changes after you read this lesson.

1. A Soulmate Is Your "Bashert"

"I didn't marry you because you were perfect. I didn't even marry you because I loved you. I married you because you gave me a promise. That promise made up for your faults. And the promise I gave you made up for mine. Two imperfect people got married and it was the promise that made the marriage. And when our children were growing up, it wasn't a house that protected them; and it wasn't our love that protected them—it was that promise."

The Yiddish word for soulmate is *bashert*, and the belief here is that, before birth, God decides who your spouse will be—a "match made in heaven." One soul is split and inhabits two bodies. Soulmates find each other, and the wedding is the joining, or *rejoining*, of souls. According to this belief, your spouse truly is your other half (maybe even your better half?), and Tom Cruise's words to Renée Zellweger in the film *Jerry Maguire* fit here: "You complete me." When my students explore this definition, they initially express despair: "What if I live in New York and my *bashert* lives in New Zealand?" Those who practice from this belief story must also have faith that destiny or divine assistance will lead them to each other's arms.

Belief in *bashert* serves as a vessel that buoys a couple during their journey of love. Couples who share a story that their union was created and is supported by a force bigger than them feel a sense of comfort, connection, and meaning. The Thornton Wilder (1942, 92–93) quote used here doesn't specifically refer to God, does it? It refers to a promise. I include the quote in this perspective because the energy feels the same to me—two people connect and remain committed to that connection because something bigger than them acts as the container or the vessel. Belief in God. Belief in remaining true to a promise. Belief acts as an anchor for your values, which then guides your thoughts and actions. If, for example, I begin to wonder what a relationship with someone else would be like, or if I begin to flirt with others out of curiosity or boredom, I can use this soulmate perspective to reconnect with what I value and what I believe. This first soulmate perspective invites faith and surrender.

2. A Soulmate Is a Fellow Traveler

"People think they have to find their soulmate to have a good marriage… Anyone you meet already has soulmates… Their mother, their father, their lifelong friends. You get married, and after twenty years of loving, bearing and raising children, and meeting challenges, then you'll have 'created' soulmate status."

This quote from Diane Sollee (2016), director of the Coalition for Marriage, Family and Couples Education, focuses on love as a journey that two people take together. Moving through space and time together *creates* the soulmate bond. The research project that highlighted greater relationship dissatisfaction among those who see soulmates as the perfect match also found that those who view soulmates as fellow travelers tended to have more adaptive perspectives on relationships. There's a joke that fits with this definition. A man approaches his rabbi and asks, "How do I know whether my wife is my soulmate?" The rabbi answers, "You know because you are married to her."

Many students have commented that this perspective takes some of the pressure off. You don't have to know whether he or she is your soulmate by the second date! What matters is whether this person is a worthy travel companion—someone with whom you can build that "relationship of constancy." As I write that sentence, I look up from my computer and see my neighbors holding hands as they walk toward their house after taking the garbage to the curb. They are in their seventies, with kids and grandkids—fellow travelers for years and years. Seeing them as I write this brings a smile to my face. Who knew taking out the trash could be so romantic?

To me this perspective feels pragmatic, loyal, and without angst. Here, there's no churning about the existential, the metaphysical, the unknown. There's no "Are we?" or "Aren't we?" It's just you and me, moving through days, months, and years together, continuing to show up because we are an "us." Lovely.

3. A Soulmate Wakes You Up

"People think a soul mate is your perfect fit, and that's what everyone wants. But a true soul mate is a mirror, the person who shows you everything that's holding you back, the person who brings you to your own attention so you can change your life. A true soul mate is probably the most important person you'll ever meet, because they tear down your walls and smack you awake. But to live with a soul mate forever? Nah. Too painful. Soul mates, they come into your life just to reveal another layer of yourself to you, and then they leave."

Elizabeth Gilbert wrote this in her wildly successful book *Eat, Pray, Love* (2007, 97). I love the wakeup call of this definition, the invitation to growth. In my experience, people tend to find her words unsettling for two reasons. First, woven into the definition is the inevitability of pain. It's not smooth sailing. You will see parts of yourself you haven't seen before. You will come face-to-face with your past, your shadow, your hiding places, your tender spots. Second, according to Gilbert, soulmate relationships are vital *and* time limited. No "till death do us part" here! A soulmate relationship creates a crisis and a crucible for transformation, allowing us to experience, in the *next* relationship, a more conscious love. Do I believe that crisis, transformation, and more-conscious love can happen all with the same partner? Of course. My relationship with Todd is living proof. As we have evolved individually and together, we have had several different marriages within our marriage.

What I also like and value about Gilbert's perspective is that rather than viewing a relationship that has ended as a *failure*, she opens the possibility of viewing a relationship that has ended as a *completion*. The relationship did what it was created to do, and now it is complete.

Soulmates Embodied

When the soulmate research mentioned earlier was published, I was asked to be part of a panel with one of the study's authors. The question for our panel was: "Should you believe in soulmates?" As I mentioned in the previous lesson, I find the question "Do you believe in X or not?" to be rather strange. The *belief* is out there already, so really the question should go something like: "Do you embrace a belief in X or not? How does a belief in X serve you or not? Does it enhance or constrain you? Open or close you? Elevate or sadden you?" My perspective was clear during that interview and remains the same today: I am 100 percent in support of you believing in soulmates *as long as* your soulmate definition includes the notion that soulmate relationships involve and invite deep, courageous, and sometimes emotionally painful work for each individual and for the couple.

Remember: you have *free will*—you can see the potential for juicy and valuable lessons inherent in a particular intimate relationship, but you get to choose whether you want to "sign up" for those lessons. Sure, any number of factors may make it difficult to exercise your free will (a particularly fateful first encounter, feelings of loneliness, powerful sexual chemistry, a whole host of "shoulds"), but it always goes back to you and your deepest truth, as you can best see, hear, and feel it in the present moment. Here's an example. On date number two, Stephanie finds out that Will spent a brief time in jail when he was nineteen years old. She is grateful that he is up-front about his history, and she feels his story of how he learned from the experience is rich and authentic (not defensive or full of rationalizations and excuses). She feels compassion for him and sees the learning that would be possible within this relationship, yet she is just not interested in "signing up" for this learning. She doesn't need to label him as a bad guy (blaming him for the relationship not working), nor does she need to beat herself up for being closed-minded (shaming herself for how she "should" be). She honors the infinite mysteries inherent in love and chooses another path.

Soulmate beliefs are there for the taking. They are not hard-and-fast rules. They are deeply personal and dynamic. Use a soulmate belief where and when it amplifies what you value and know to be your deepest truth today. Release the belief when and if it acts like an emotional prison. Bring awareness to what you believe at this moment in time, witnessing whether and how it works for you.

Steps Toward Loving Bravely

Your beliefs about soulmates shape how you approach an intimate relationship.

Working Definition

Journal about how you define soulmates. Before reading this lesson, what did you believe about soulmates? Which of the soulmate descriptions in this lesson resonates with you the most? Why? Which of the soulmate descriptions in this lesson do you find yourself resisting the most? Why?

Breaking Open

Write down the names of three people you feel close to: intimate partner, friend, and/or family member. Under each name, create a list of lessons learned from him or her. Make another list of what you think that person has learned from being in a relationship with you. To what degree do any or all of these feel like soulmate relationships? Why or why not?

Soulmates in Action

Reach out to someone you feel close to—a friend, a sibling, or an ex—and ask what his or her relationship with you has taught him or her about him- or herself. Here are some questions you could ask:

What did you learn about yourself from our relationship?
In what ways do you feel that I am a teacher to you?

In what ways do you feel that you are a teacher to me?

What is your perspective on soulmates?

To what extent does our relationship feel like a soulmate relationship to you?

Lesson 9

Listen to Your Gut

The compass of the entire universe is within you.

—Wayne Dyer

You'd be surprised to know how much time I spend during therapy sessions and lectures pointing to my belly. The belly plays such a critical role in intimate relationships that we are going to dedicate an entire lesson to the vital data that comes from... the belly. I'm talking, of course, about intuition, or gut feelings. There are certainly times when you need to rely on your *head* in order to *think* your way through a situation. And there are certainly times when you need to rely on your *heart* in order to *feel* your way through a situation. But you may underestimate the value of relying on your *gut* in order to *sense* your way through a situation.

Red Light, Green Light

As adults, we take in great quantities of external noise about who we "should" be and how we "should" live. Our world is chock-full of judgments and opinions and advice. This noise can be so loud, in fact, that it is nearly impossible to hear ourselves from within. But I don't think we start off unable to tune in to ourselves.

I remember playing Chutes and Ladders with my daughter Courtney when she was about six years old. She pulled a fast one, moving her piece an extra spot in order to avoid a dreaded big slide that would knock her from nearly the finish line to nearly the start. I watched her do it, and I could see her choice written all over her sheepish freckled face. I was at a parental crossroads as I contemplated my next move. Luckily, I was experiencing a moment of mama-clarity. I took my turn, quietly and with a neutral face, as I could tell that she was standing at her own crossroads. Within a minute or so, she said quietly, "Mommy, I cheated a little." I asked her to take a deep breath and be still for a moment, and then said, "Courtney, I'm so glad you're telling me this. Tell me, how did cheating feel in your body?" "Bad," she said. "Where did you feel that bad feeling?" "Right here," she said, pointing to her belly.

I talked to her for a moment about "green light" feelings and "red light" feelings. "Green light" feelings tell you that the choices you're making are healthy and aligned with the person you are and want to be. "Red light" feelings tell you that the choices you're making don't serve you very well and probably aren't best for you. The sense she got in her belly was clearly a red light feeling.

Did I punish her? Nope. Any desire to teach her some abstract (and external) lesson about how she *should* behave was trumped by my desire to strengthen her ability to tune in to herself, as I trust that she came into this world with an internal compass. Her life will afford her many moments of choice, and I won't always be there to praise her "green light" choices and give consequences for her "red light" choices. What *will* always be there is her gut.

Bodily Truth

It's called a "visceral" feeling or reaction for a reason. Your viscera (stomach and intestines) have nerve cells (neurons) that send data, via a lightning-fast neural pathway called lamina I in your spinal cord, up to your brain. Most of us think of the brain as the central processing unit that tells the rest of the body what to do, but this finding affirms what we intuitively know: We obtain valuable information from the bottom up! It's the sense you get that someone is looking at you. The chill in your spine when someone is being dishonest or malicious. The twisting-up feeling you get when you're saying yes but you really mean no. It's the feeling that Courtney had in her belly when she cheated at Chutes and Ladders.

Beyond the brilliant biology of gut feelings, there's something else at work. Let's look at the Dr. Wayne Dyer quote from the beginning of this lesson: "The compass of the entire universe is within you." Entire books have been written about this idea of collective wisdom or the intelligence of the universe. Each of us is connected to that vast collective wisdom, and we can source it for comfort and guidance.

I have been a provider and consumer of traditional psychotherapy for many years, and it has benefited me tremendously. Since I was in my twenties, I have also dabbled in spirituality—read a book here, attended a workshop there. In recent years, I have become deeply committed to bringing my spiritual self into everything I do, and I can say with confidence it has been nothing short of life-changing for me! By widening my lens to honor what is beyond the world of our five senses, I am better able to handle stress; I feel more connected to my husband, friends, and family; and I trust life a whole lot more than I used to. Whether or not you integrate religious or spiritual practice into your life today, I suspect you have had experiences of tapping into whatever it is that is bigger, wiser, and older than we are. I feel connected to this big universal energy frequently because I value making time and space to consciously connect—but long before I valued "seeking," those experiences found me anyway. I am guessing they find you too.

I remember being on vacation with my family one time when I was going through a difficult breakup. I walked down to the rocks on the lake while everyone was sleeping. The moonlight on the water sparkled like diamonds. I cried for a while and then felt strangely calm—held, safe, and connected to something bigger and wiser than me. I was *both* heartbroken *and* safe. Similarly, when my dad passed away a few years ago, trusting something bigger than I am helped me ride huge waves of grief while also experiencing the joy of memories of him and a renewed gratitude for life. For me, holding on to both/and—in this case, grief and joy—is much easier to do when the dialectic is supercharged or wrapped in connection to greater mystery and wisdom. Sometimes that gut-level knowing guides our actions (trust this person, quit this job, and so forth), but sometimes that gut-level knowing just reminds us that we can endure a particularly dark chapter.

Love in Phone World

Regardless of whether you think about your gut feelings as pure biology or as biology mixed with something divine, your ability to listen to and respect your gut impacts your love life from the first date on. It's a big part of why I am suspicious about relationships that largely exist in what comedian and author Aziz Ansari calls "phone world" (2015). Especially as you're getting to know someone, one-dimensional, screen-based communication compromises your ability to make use of your most powerful relational tool—your gut. It's very hard to sense, in that deep visceral way, how you feel with someone unless you are both in the same space at the same time. In our high-tech, fast-paced, information-heavy digital age, we must remember and honor our oldest and wisest tool of discernment.

One of my clients was in a long-distance relationship with a guy she really liked. He cheated on her a few months into the relationship. Both of them desperately wanted to stay together, and they were trying hard to rebuild trust. Despite hours communicating via text and FaceTime, she could not let him back in. There were multiple factors at work, but at some point I reflected to her how truly difficult it must be to rebuild trust without being in the same space at the same time. His words were sincere, his behavior was congruent, but she could not *feel* him. Her head could take in his words. Her heart could be full of love for him. But without being able to involve all of her senses, it seemed her viscera simply could not cooperate. I felt grateful that she took her emotions seriously, as agreeing to rebuild with a gnawing feeling inside would have felt like a dishonoring of self. They ultimately made the courageous and difficult choice to let each other go.

Listening to Yourself

Sadly, even though we are gifted deep inner wisdom at birth, it is all too easy to lose contact with this potent data source. The noise of the external world gets so loud. We are told in a myriad of ways that we need outside sets of rules to follow, and that, if left to our own devices, we will be out of control, dangerous, and destructive. As children, we are told in so many ways (by parents, schools, and religious institutions), "I know better than you what's best for you." Dating and relationship books that offer rules and formulas for success are both seductive and risky. What if following someone else's recipe requires you to further disconnect from your compass?

If you identify as a "people pleaser," you likely ignore your gut feelings on the regular. Symptoms of ignoring gut feelings include resentment; slow, simmering anger; a sense of internal flatness; and boredom. There's a gender socialization piece here as well. Girls and women (more so than boys and men) are praised and rewarded for being nice, agreeable, and accommodating, which may make it more natural to ignore our internal signals to act otherwise.

I get it. Gut feelings can be quite inconvenient. I was recently asked to do something at work. I really wanted to say yes because I could tell that the person asking really wanted me to say yes. Unfortunately, I could feel, clear as can be, within my gut that my deepest truth was "No, I am not able to do that at this time." I tried to look at the situation in different ways, using my head (*What if I... Maybe I could...*). I could also hear a variety of internalized and old stories from the outside world playing inside my head (*A good employee would... You should... People will be mad if you don't...*). Despite all of this internal drama, my gut would not relent. Every time I imagined saying yes, my gut tightened in a familiar way. So I said no, and I survived the consequences. If I had made the choice to be a people pleaser, I would undoubtedly have experienced the symptoms of having ignored a gut feeling: resentment and dread. Yet, saying no was tough because it meant disappointing someone.

"What If My Gut Feeling Is to Punch Someone in the Face?"

I was recently teaching the idea of listening to your gut to a group of students, and a guy asked me the above question. Basically, he was asking whether you can justify any behavior by claiming that it was your gut feeling. No. It doesn't work like that. Wanting to punch someone in the face is a reflection of being emotionally triggered: fired up, set off, upset in the moment. When triggered, it is hard (dare I say impossible?) to access deep inner knowing. Emotions swirl, and the internal buzz drowns out intuition. Intense negative feelings are a cue to stop and begin an all-hands-on-deck effort to slow down and quiet down before making a next move. From an empowered (not triggered) place, you can then be curious about your reactivity, asking, "What is the story I am telling myself about the situation?" This question invites depth—depth that reaches down to your gut, the root of knowing. From that deeper and quieter space within, multiple paths emerge, indicating next steps you might want or need to take. In all likelihood, none of those paths will involve punching someone in the face.

"Is It Anxiety, or Is It a Gut Feeling?"

I remember putting our wedding invitations in the mail and promptly freaking out. Sweaty palms, racing heart, and thoughts like, "What am I getting myself into?" flooded me. Was this anxiety or a gut feeling? Sometimes it is hard to tell.

Yet, if you can bring some awareness to your reactions, you can learn how anxious feelings and gut feelings show up in their own ways in your body. Discerning the difference can guide your course of action. To me (and many others), anxiety feels like tightness in my chest and pressure in my head. Anxious, frantic thoughts and stories flood and swirl around in my brain. By contrast, data that comes from my gut feels more raw, primary, and unfiltered. And what's become especially noticeable to me is how I feel when I ignore my gut. That feeling is a low, slow tightening or twisting of my insides.

In this case of the wedding invitations, anxiety would have been nervousness about the magnitude of my decision to marry Todd. A gut feeling would have been a deep inner knowing that I was making a "red light" choice. Ultimately deciding that my freak-out was a result of anxiety led me to work on calming myself down and talking with people I trust about how nervous I was feeling. If I had decided that my freak-out was in fact a gut feeling, it might have led me to reconsider marrying Todd.

When my clients are sitting with this question, we work together on quieting their bodies and minds so they can carefully attend to what is happening within. Sometimes, a client's relationship doubts are a reflection of fear-based old stories about the self ("I can't believe that someone would really stay with me. I'm worthless."), but sometimes a client's relationship doubts indicate that something truly is amiss in the relationship. A sense that "something doesn't feel right" certainly warrants exploration. For a summary of the work of this lesson, you can go online and download the handout "How to Listen to Your Gut and Why" (at http://www.newharbinger.com/35814).

Steps Toward Loving Bravely

Brave relationship choices require trusting the vital information that comes from your intuitive knowing, your gut.

Family Voice

Write a journal entry about how your family of origin related to your gut feelings. In what ways did your family *honor* your inner knowing, giving you the message "You are wise and your inner voice should be honored"? In what ways did your family's dynamics take you out of contact with your inner voice, giving you the message "We know what's best for you"? This is complicated, of course, as all kids need guidance, instruction, and support from the adults in their lives. But some parents find ways to celebrate their child's inner wisdom while also holding boundaries and setting limits. How did your parents navigate this?

Listening from Within

It's important to be able to discern anxiety versus intuition, so practice tuning in to yourself. The next time you are approaching a decision, quiet down and pay attention to your insides before making your choice. Learn—or, more accurately, *remember*—how your gut feelings talk to you. What is your gut saying to you as you stand at this crossroads?

First, practice pausing and listening to your intuitive voice with small decisions: "What do I want to order for dinner?" "Should I go out or stay home tonight?" Can you hear the voice that speaks to you from underneath the "should"? In what ways does it speak differently than the voice of shoulds? How do you feel when you obey the voice of should? How do you feel when you honor your gut-level feeling? How are those two feelings different?

As you feel comfortable listening to your deep knowing when you make small decisions, try listening to your deep knowing as you face large decisions as well: "Do I want a second date with this person?" "What would it be like to ask the person I'm dating how serious she wants to be?" "How well is this job serving me?" Try to listen for the voice of should and the voice of your gut.

Source Your Life

Tell me, what is it you plan to do with your one wild and precious life?

—Mary Oliver

Some years back, I had an "aha" moment that was really good for me and for my intimate relationship. Todd and I participated in a fund-raising walk in downtown Chicago for a national autism organization. The walk ended on Soldier Field (home of the Chicago Bears), where there was live music, and kids and families could run, dance, and toss a football to their hearts' content. To my football-obsessed husband, this was a dream come true. At some point, we walked up into the stands to observe the scene from above. Todd put his arm around me and said, "This is my temple. It has been my temple since I was a kid." In that moment, I got it, and I surrendered the final remnants of my long-standing rivalry with the Chicago Bears.

Like many intimate partners, I tended to, in insecure moments, perceive Todd's passion for football as a slight against me. I was prone, for many years, to telling myself a thin and unhelpful story about a love triangle between Todd, da Bears, and me. My story was that the time he spent with *them* took something away from *me*. Sure, we found ways to muddle through. We tried pragmatic accommodations: me watching with him (bust), him skipping an occasional game to be with me (bust). We tried emotional accommodations: I could talk myself through my icky feelings, and he had ways of reassuring me of my importance to him. But it wasn't until I sat in the stands with him, on that sunny May afternoon, that I actually *transformed* my story, once and for all. Seeing through *his* eyes, my story thickened up, allowing me to transcend my fears and the accompanying judgments, and deeply and humbly feel all of what football means to him. Soldier Field is where he goes to connect to his brothers, the memory of his father, and the tribe that is all of Bears fans. It's old, primal, and, quite frankly, none of my business. Todd without the Bears would cease to be Todd. In my "aha" moment, I was able to see that I am *fortunate* that the man I love knows how to access his deep passion, to stoke his fire. It is good for him. It is good for us.

Passionate Living

A rich and meaningful love story is best crafted by those committed to living with passion—those who know how to *source* their lives (Oriah 1999). Sourcing your life is about feeding yourself from within. This lesson invites you to ask yourself an essential question: **What do I need present in my life in order to feel alive, joyful, and passionate?**

Intimate partners do not necessarily share or need to share those passions. My passions are uniquely mine. Your passions are uniquely yours. It is often the case that intimate partners turn away from the relationship and engage their passion, allowing them to return to the relationship more openhearted, alive, and engaged. Loving bravely means working to support passionate living—for yourself and for your partner.

Professor and writer Iris Krasnow (2011) interviewed more than two hundred wives to learn more about their experiences in married life, and she was struck by how many of them credited their relationship success to an outside hobby or passion, often one rediscovered or carried over from childhood (dance, horseback riding, and so on). She found that those who stoked their fires from within felt happier in their marriages. Bringing burnt-out, self-sacrificing, crusty energy to the relationship does not serve anyone. It is a recipe for resentment.

Much more than "free time" or "downtime," engaging your passion is key for emotional wellness, deepening and supporting your relationship with *yourself.* Knowing what "turns you on" is an important aspect of relational self-awareness. Likely there is a menu of practices and activities that help you access your source: a thirty-minute walk with a special playlist that calms and opens you, working on your motorcycle at the end of a long day, or a weekend retreat. Solitude and intimacy are inextricably bound, with each feeding the other. Turning inward and connecting to ourselves readies us to turn outward and connect with others.

Getting Curious

If you feel resistant to the idea that couples ought to have passions and hobbies outside of their primary relationship, holding on to the idea that "love ought to be enough," it is worth asking yourself *What keeps me from embracing the idea that partners need and benefit from pursuing passions outside of the relationship?* Old stories may be getting in the way, leading you to equate turning away in order to refuel, restore, or recharge with turning away in order to abandon or betray. Perhaps the old story is, "I ought to be enough for him or her," so the other person's passion feels like a slap in the face, putting you in direct contact with feelings of shame and inadequacy.

If you find yourself feeling judgmental about your intimate partner's outside passion, it is worth asking yourself: *What frightens, worries, or upsets me about my partner's outside passion?* One client of mine was dating a woman who was an avid tennis player. He found himself irritated and hurt when she played, wishing she would opt for time with him instead. He was able to move from a reactive place (making snippy comments to her or shutting down emotionally on the nights she played) to a curious place by asking himself the above question. It was helpful for him to explore the stories he was telling himself about what her playing must mean about her feelings for him, mostly: "I must not matter very much to her." From this brave place of self-awareness, he could share with her the complexity of his feelings. This allowed them to create work-arounds that felt win-win: she made extra effort to verbalize her love for him, and they scheduled additional time to hang out together.

Outside passions merit relational support, yet at times the passion may directly threaten the integrity of the intimate relationship. For one couple I saw in therapy, his passion for erotic photography felt to her like a violation, so we worked together to find a way for him to honor *both* his artistic passion *and* his marriage. This dynamic had many layers of complexity, but I bring it up here as a reminder that simple rules rarely do the trick when it comes to love.

If you find yourself holding back from pursuing your passions, ask yourself: *What is the story I tell myself about my passions? In what ways do I fear my passions will threaten my love life?* Another client of mine felt afraid to find a bible study community for fear that her desire to pursue her faith would drive her partner away. Whenever we bump up against those thin, either/or stories, it is an opportunity to seek out the both/and: *How can I celebrate* both *my passion and my relationship?*

Tribal Membership

Cultural stories about how our romantic partner ought to fulfill our every need (partner, coparent, lover, best friend) can get us into lots of trouble. Our expectations get set far too high, and disappointment is inevitable. Certainly, it is reasonable to expect emotional intimacy, conversation, and mutual support within an intimate relationship, but expecting *all* of your support to come from your intimate partner sets you up to feel let down.

Single or partnered, we always need a *tribe*—treasured and trusted friends who see us in our fullness and folly and love us anyway. Krasnow (2016) found that "the wives with the highest marital satisfaction have a tight circle of wild and warm women friends with whom to drink, travel and vent." Men need this too! The best tribes are those that serve love—honoring vulnerability and struggle, holding space for emotional pain (resisting the urge to rescue or appease), and offering feedback, opinions, and advice only when asked.

What about a tribe that doesn't serve love? For example, a therapy client of mine wanted desperately to be faithful to her boyfriend, but two of her close friends were cheating on theirs. Yes, she has free will, but she was wise to be curious about the impact of their choices on her. Some friendships foster and enable behaviors that undermine an intimate relationship, and if that is the case, it can be clarifying to look within and bravely ask: *What part of me is served by participating in a friendship that compromises my ability to show up fully for my intimate relationship?*

Work with Purpose

In addition to passions and friendships, work can be soul-feeding and purposeful. It is certainly the case that one can be unhappy in his or her work life and happy in his or her love life, but dissatisfaction with work warrants attention because the ripple effect can be damaging. Work that feels exploitive (of you or others) or that you have chosen because it was someone else's dream for you can be incredibly draining, compromising your self-esteem and outlook on life. There can be subtle yet powerful ways that work influences love and love influences work, so bringing your awareness to that intersection can be illuminating. Ask yourself: *How does my work shape my current experience of my love life? How does the current status of my love life impact my work?*

If your work is negatively affecting your love life, it is worth asking yourself: *What is the story I am telling myself about working this job I hate? What is getting in the way of me making a change? What feels frightening about imagining making a change?*

The opening quote of this lesson invites us to think about what we will do with this one wild and precious life. A fulfilling intimate relationship certainly tops most of our lists, as love is a rich source of meaning. But love is not our only source, and we need to find purpose through passions, through friendships, and through work. Being committed to living with passion serves you now and always, and it serves love too.

Steps Toward Loving Bravely

In the creation of a "we," devote time, space, and energy to the "me."

Life Playlist

Here's a throwback reference for you. In the 1990s TV show *Ally McBeal*, Ally was going through a difficult time, and her therapist told her that she needed a theme song for her life. This episode stayed with me because, for so many of us, music plays a sacred role in our emotional and relational lives. I can't say that I have one theme song for my life. What I do have is a playlist that I can use as needed. I rely on music to:

- Honor and deepen a sad feeling I am moving through
- Energize me when I feel low
- Embolden me before an important event
- Connect me with others (family dance party)
- Transition me to special couple time (wink, wink)

Music can help you tap into your source, connecting you to what fuels, drives, and sustains you. Do you have a theme song? What songs are on your life playlist? If you don't already use music in this way, identify some songs you connect with and use them when you need to deepen or shift what's going on inside of you.

What's on Your Platter?

Because how you take care of yourself has a direct impact on your love life, it is worth taking a look at what's on your *platter*. Doctors David Rock and Daniel Siegel (2011) created the Healthy Mind Platter as a takeoff on the United States government's revamped food pyramid. Rather than focusing on the foods we eat, the Healthy Mind Platter identifies seven daily activities that "make up the full set of 'mental nutrients' that your brain needs to function at its best." The seven are:

- Focus time (to be goal-oriented)

- Playtime (to be spontaneous and creative)

- Connecting time (to connect self to others and/or self to nature)

- Physical time (to move our bodies)

- Time in (to reflect inward)

- Down time (to be nonfocused and/or to recharge)

- Sleep time (zzzz)

When you engage in each of these activities daily, "you enable your brain to coordinate and balance its activities, which strengthens your brain's internal connections and your connections with other people" (2011).

There are no specific guidelines for how much time makes up "a serving" of each of these. Think about how you spent your time during the past three days by answering the following questions.

How much of each of these mental nutrients did you get?

Were any omitted altogether, showing you which areas of your life you are currently neglecting? Which do you need more of?

How could you shift your priorities in order to dedicate time to areas in which you are "malnourished"?

Tapping Your Source

What do you feel passionate about? Write down three hobbies or other activities that have been or are part of your life, and then answer the following questions:

> Which mental nutrients do these activities give you?
>
> How do you feel when you are engaged in these activities?
>
> What do these activities say about you as a person?
>
> How do you feel when these activities are *not* part of your daily, weekly, monthly, or annual routine?
>
> What is the relationship between your love life and your passion? In what ways does (or could) your area of passion serve, help, or bolster your intimate relationship?

Note: If your activity or passion isn't creative, take a moment to think about the role of creativity in your life. Many of us (myself included) have a story of self that says, "I am not creative." In fact, all of us are, and we are most whole and connected when we are involved in a creative process of some kind. Feeding your creativity feeds your intimate relationship. Creativity is defined very broadly here: building, decorating, writing, dancing, gardening, cooking, repairing, singing, landscaping, and so on. In what ways do you honor creativity in your life?

The "Me" in "We"

Have you had the experience of feeling threatened by or judgmental about your intimate partner's hobby or activity? If so, answer the following questions in a journal entry:

> What are the feelings you experienced in relation to your partner's hobby (anger, envy, sadness)?
>
> In what ways are these feelings tied to the core issues you identified in Lesson 2?

Does this issue remind you of a dynamic or a story from your past?

What does your triggered feeling tell you about the state of the relationship?

Have you had the experience of an intimate partner feeling threatened by or feeling judgmental about *your* passion, hobby, or favorite activity? If so, answer the following questions in a journal entry:

How did you feel when you were faced with your partner's judgment about your passion?

How did you handle your partner's judgmental feelings?

Were you able to see ways that your partner's judgments reflected his or her core issues? Are you able to see that now?

What might help you honor *both* your partner's core issue *and* your need to pursue your passion?

PART 3

Self-Expression

Lesson 11

Inhabit Your Body

Erotic intimacy holds the double promise of finding oneself and losing oneself. It is an experience of merger and of total self-absorption, of mutuality and selfishness.

—Esther Perel

The body. Oh, the body! A book about self-awareness in the service of love must make space for the body. Touch, affection, and sex are integral aspects of being human, and they are essential forms of communication within an intimate relationship. Giving and receiving pleasure through the body grows, reflects, and sustains love. All touch, but especially sexual touch, requires a willingness to get naked—emotionally and physically—putting us in contact with deep truths about who we are and who we want to be. Although touch happens in the space *between* two people, happy sex begins with a compassionate and loving relationship with the self. Therefore, this lesson is about how to know and appreciate your *erotic self*—who you are sexually—in order to maximize your enjoyment of sex as a vital element of an intimate relationship.

For starters, you need to know what emotions you're bringing into bed with you. The bawdy and bodacious actress Mae West famously referred to sex as "emotion in motion." In fact, all touch—cuddling, affectionate touch, and sexual touch—is emotion in motion. Touch is an avenue for manifesting, embodying, and expressing to and with another person what we are feeling on the inside. Like an iceberg, the above-the-surface aspects of touch appear rather straightforward—a body in connection with another body. But there's a whole lot more happening beneath the surface. Touch is both simple and complicated. Our reactions to touching and being touched can be quite profound, and our reactions offer us direct access to our deepest longings, stories, hopes, fears, and truths. *Our reactions to touching and being touched are full of data that deserves our attention.*

Like most aspects of our intimate lives, how we react to touch dates back to a time long before we were sexually active. As mammals, touch feeds, nurtures, and shapes us from our first breath to our last. The touch we received (or didn't) from our caregivers taught us potent lessons about worthiness, closeness, safety, and soothing. If we were touched in ways that were gentle and respectful, our bodies learned to feel safe and relaxed in the presence of others. If touch was absent, minimal, or disrespectful, our bodies learned to feel defensive and on edge in the presence of others.

Later, as sexuality blossoms, those early experiences are the template upon which our journey into sexual touch maps. Sex becomes another venue for expressing ourselves, and sex is another way of feeling close to others and feeling valued by them. Yet sex never replaces our continued need and desire for affectionate touch and cozy touch. Kissing hello and good-bye, snuggling on the couch while watching a movie, holding hands during a walk—these kinds of physical interactions are related to *and* separate from sexual touch. All avenues of touch entwine, and all have a place.

How have you experienced touch in your life? Telling your "touch story" is illuminative and healing, and you will be supported in doing so at the end of this lesson. Although sexual intimacy is an important element of an intimate relationship, it is an element that is tender and complicated. We will never eliminate the complexities of sexual intimacy—and we wouldn't want to—but self-awareness helps us navigate those intricacies.

Self-Aware Sex

Having a brave relationship with your sexual self is the work of a lifetime. Because our bodies and our minds are ever-changing, who we are sexually continues to develop from adolescence to old age. The work of sexual self-awareness simply can't ever be *done*, because we are moving targets. In addition, it is very difficult to be whole-hearted and self-aware sexually in a culture that has a confusing relationship with sex. In lesson 6 we explored how cultural messages shape how we feel about ourselves. The messages we receive about who we should be sexually are loud and, quite frankly, incoherent. Companies use sex to sell everything from cars to hamburgers. Pornography can be accessed from our phones in the blink of an eye, anywhere, anytime. Religious institutions, schools, and families tend to talk about sex in simplistic black-and-white terms that leave no room for the many shades of gray that we tend to feel when it comes to sex. In this chaotic atmosphere, it is *really* hard to hear what is inside of us.

How many of us have received a wholehearted and comprehensive sexual education? Most of the clients I work with and students I teach have simply never been granted time and space to understand themselves sexually. The lucky ones learned the basics about reproduction, STIs, sexual assault, and sexual abuse, but that curriculum leaves much unsaid. It's still about taking information in from the outside, rather than being taught how to listen to yourself from the inside. When it comes to sex, there are so many questions that can be answered from one place and one place only: *within you*. These worthwhile questions include:

How does my relationship with my body affect how I feel sexually?

How do I define "sexy"?

What turns me on?

What are the ingredients for a "good" and fulfilling sexual experience with another person?

What do I believe about the role of sex in an intimate relationship?

Each and every one of us deserves the opportunity to think about, and to feel about, these kinds of questions.

But the journey can't stop there. In an intimate relationship, two people, each with their own sexual story and sexual template, create something together. That creation is informed by each individual's desires, ideas, and beliefs. As the quote from Esther Perel, author of *Mating in Captivity: Unlocking Erotic Intelligence*, at the beginning of this lesson suggests, sex is simultaneously selfish and selfless (2007). It's a conversation of sorts with self and other, at the very same time. The quality of your "conversation" with your partner is shaped by the quality of the conversation you are having with yourself. And the conversation that your partner is having with him- or herself surely shapes your sexual experience too! Therefore, it is an important relationship skill to be able to listen to your partner's sexual truths.

A client recently shared with me that he tried to open up to his wife about a sexual worry he was having. He felt it was taking longer for him to become erect, and his erection was feeling "less reliable" to him. He reported that she responded by giggling and rolling her eyes. It seems that his vulnerable self-disclosure triggered discomfort in her, leading her to respond in a dismissive way. Even when it feels uncomfortable to meet your partner's sexual truth with openness, intimacy depends on your ability to do so. My hope is that she will explore the story she began to tell herself when she was confronted by what he shared.

Sexual self-awareness is vital, as it lays the foundation for the creation of self-aware sex—sex that is mindful, intentional, and conscious. Sex that is brave! Here are some qualities that capture a *self-aware sexual experience*:

- I am in the present moment (versus lost in the past or worrying about what's next).

- I am in touch with my body.

- I feel able to communicate what I want and need.

- I feel emotionally and physically connected to myself.

- I feel emotionally and physically connected to my partner.

In contrast, here are some qualities of a sexual experience that happens in the absence of self-awareness:

- I am lost in the past. (Memories are troubling me.)

- I am worried about the future or distracted by other thoughts.

- I am not in touch with my body. (I am not sure what I am feeling… I am under the influence of alcohol or drugs that compromise my ability to "hear" myself.)

- I don't feel able to communicate what I want and need (because I am afraid, self-conscious, or uncomfortable, or because I don't know how).

- I am not emotionally connected with myself. (I am pushing down my emotions… I feel emotionally numb.)

- I am not emotionally connected with my partner. (I feel distant, disengaged, or emotionally unsafe.)

These are qualities to ponder rather than hard-and-fast rules, and they are offered in the service of reflection. Moving toward creating and engaging in sexual experiences that are brave, mindful, intentional, and conscious begins by naming what is getting in your way. For the rest of this lesson, we will explore some practices that can move you toward greater sexual self-awareness. The "Guide to Self-Aware Sex" at http://www.newharbinger.com/35814 contains tips, suggestions, and additional resources for a happy and healthy sex life.

Question Hookup Culture

In my work with young adults in the classroom and the therapy room, I spend a lot of time talking about "hookup culture," and, as it is usually practiced today, hookup culture is a barrier to brave and self-aware sex. By way of definition, a hookup has three elements:

- A hookup includes some form of sexual intimacy, anything from kissing to oral, vaginal, or anal sex—and everything in between. The term "hooking up" is an enormous and intentionally vague umbrella.

- A hookup is brief. It can be as short as a few minutes to as long as several hours during a single night.

- A hookup is intended to be purely physical in nature and involves both parties shutting down any communication or connection that might lead to emotional attachment. (Freitas 2013, 25)

Hooking up is not new. My friends and I engaged in a hookup or two while we were college students in the 1990s…while wearing oversize flannel and listening to Pearl Jam. But today's young adults have taken it to a whole new level. It seems that today's hookups involve more alcohol—students often talk about being "blackout drunk" as if it's normal or common. It seems that today's hookups involve more sex (versus a dance-floor makeout). Finally, it seems that hooking up is the predominant form of coupling, whereas in the 1990s we saw lots of couples in exclusive or committed relationships (Solomon 2016).

A number of forces converge to create and maintain hookup culture:

- People are getting married later than ever and therefore simply have more years to explore multiple intimate relationships.

- There is a sense of doubt and fear regarding the institution of marriage that can lead people to seek casual and brief relationships.

- Living in the digital age profoundly shapes every aspect of our intimate relationships, offering us the illusion that we can keep our relationships neat and tidy by handling much of the business of love via social media. Behind our screens, we can ponder, edit, and plan. Face-to-face, we cannot.

Hookups feel like an extension of the wish that love could be simple and easy—and therefore not painful. Hookup culture reflects a fear of getting entangled, a fear of getting hurt, and a fear of screwing up. In this way, hookup culture is an effort to stay emotionally safe, reflecting *and* perpetuating anxiety, ambivalence, and pessimism about love.

But there is a cost that comes along with clinging to a story that love ought to be "chill." When you operate under this belief, you are required to ignore the many emotional layers that exist beneath the facade of "chill." Woven into the story of the hookup scene is shame when someone "catches feelings." To catch feelings is to fail! When I am talking with students or clients, and they express disappointment and shame that they fell for the person they were supposed to be just hooking up with, my response tends to be, "Of course you did! Sex is powerful magic." We fancy ourselves to be high-tech and evolved, but we are hardwired to emotionally connect to those whose bodies we dive into via sex. Orgasm triggers oxytocin, the "cuddle hormone" of attachment, so it is cruel to reprimand yourself for catching feelings despite your intention to keep it easy breezy. The very situation has you set up to fail!

A hookup is usually neither a cocreated nor an honest contract. Often both people are drunk and/or high during the hookup, and, as mentioned above, being under the influence of alcohol or drugs compromises your ability to fully participate in a sexual experience. It can even compromise the ability to affirmatively give and receive sexual consent, meaning that a hookup can be more than just unconscious or mindless. It can be a sexual assault.

A hookup is also not a cocreated and honest contract when *intentions* are misaligned. Many people (especially women) have shared with me that hooking up feels like the only avenue into an intimate relationship. People participate in a hookup in the hope that an intimate relationship will result—giving sex to get love. Sometimes hooking up *does* lead to an intimate relationship. However, since disconnection from self seems to be a prerequisite to hooking up, this gamble seems awfully risky.

It is, of course, possible to create conscious, aligned, and authentic sexual experiences outside of the context of a committed intimate relationship. From a place of self-awareness, you may choose to engage in a sexual experience in the service of adventure, curiosity, play, and/or growth. This is different than hookup sex. A student of mine, Mitch, is an example of this.

Despite having his family's support and the support of his friends when he came out as gay in high school, Mitch spent his college years on an emotional roller coaster. He felt "obsessed" with the idea that he shouldn't hook up because that would fulfill the stereotype of the promiscuous gay guy. Instead, he thought he ought to *only* be interested in a serious intimate relationship. But he struggled to find a guy to date, so he would get drunk, make out with someone, and then feel awful about it for weeks.

Today, at twenty-four years old, Mitch is still single, and he decided to experiment with casual sex. He met someone on a hookup app. Before meeting, they talked on the phone and said out loud to each other that all they were interested in was sex—they cocreated an honest contract. He went to his house completely sober. They talked for a few minutes and then had sex. "I was interested in *my* experience," Mitch told me. "If he had fun too, that was even better, but this was about me. If the sex was bad or if I felt uncomfortable at any point, I knew I could have stopped it and left. I'd never have to see him again if I didn't want to. It turned out to be a great experience that helped me understand myself better sexually. Afterward, I got in my car, called my best friend, and declared, 'I'm in my sexual renaissance.'" Mitch's experience has all the elements of a self-aware sexual experience even though it occurred outside of a committed intimate relationship.

Love Your Body

Body image concerns pull you out of your present-moment experience, dampening the pleasures of sex. Celebrating the body you live in, *exactly as it is today*, can help you leave your self-critical voice behind so you can show up for fun! Our minds and bodies are intricately connected, so judgmental thoughts about yourself—"My belly is too fat"; "My hips are too wide"—get in the way of physical pleasure. Stopping negative self-talk is easier said than done, but recognizing that you are having negative thoughts is a vital first step! You are not your thoughts, so start by *naming* negative thoughts as they creep in during sex. For example, you have the thought, "My belly is so fat." Train yourself to have this thought next: "I am not the negative thought I just had."

Once you have recognized that you are having a negative thought, you can make the choice to transform it. You will have to play around and see what works for you. Perhaps imagine plucking the negative thought like a weed and sending it down a river. Replace the thought with a loving and affirming thought about yourself (such as "I am strong," "I am worthy," or "I am beautiful"), and bring your attention back to the present moment. Feel your partner's skin against yours. Focus on where your body is feeling pleasure, and imagine that feeling growing and spreading through your body. When it comes to sex, there are plenty of exciting places to put your attention—places more worthy of your attention than negative self talk!

Shed Old Sexual Stories

If you grew up being told that sex is bad, dangerous, or dirty, those old stories can play in your head during sex, making it difficult to let go and seek out or surrender to pleasurable sensations. Much as we did earlier in this lesson with negative self-talk about body image, it is really helpful to name those stories as such—old stories that once had a time and a place in your life but that do not serve you in the context of your intimate relationship today. Create a new story for yourself about how good sex *enhances* your life. You are *entitled* to pleasure, play, escape, and erotic connection with another person.

Own Your Pleasure

Unfortunately, it's difficult for many of us to feel entitled to pleasure. Feeling good can feel bad. Sometimes old messages about seeking pleasure as greedy, selfish, and "too much" can make you feel bad about wanting to feel good. If you feel uncomfortable declaring that you are worthy of pleasure, you may not feel okay doing what it takes to understand how your body works and what feels good for you, and this may manifest in hesitation around exploring masturbation or giving feedback to your partner.

For a number of reasons, women are especially at risk of minimizing the importance of their own pleasure. They may wait silently and passively for an orgasm to arrive. They may end up faking an orgasm because they feel guilty about how long it's taking or ashamed of not being able to get there. Faking orgasms is an attempted solution to a difficult problem but with unintended consequences. People usually fake orgasms in order to keep the peace and/or to protect their partner's feelings, both of which are noble intentions. Even if your faked orgasm smoothes the moment over, the long-term consequences can include compromised sexual desire, resentment, and a nagging sense of dishonesty in your intimate relationship.

You deserve to learn what works for your body, and you deserve to be able to talk with your partner about what makes you feel good. If advocating for yourself sexually feels frightening, embarrassing, or hurtful, return to the previous practice (Shed Old Sexual Stories) and uproot the old story that supports the idea that silently waiting or faking beats self-advocacy.

Be Discerning About Erotic Materials

Reaching for erotic materials is common. Pornography is a multibillion-dollar industry, and the *Fifty Shades of Grey* series of books has sold more than one hundred million copies worldwide (Bosman 2014). Throw in Nicholas Sparks books and movies, and you've got the economy of a small nation! What fuels our desire to turn outside of ourselves and our relationship for sexual inspiration and arousal is a book unto itself. When a sexual partner is unavailable, erotic materials can fill a void. When couples are curious to explore, watching something sexy together can reduce self-consciousness and heighten excitement. But caution is warranted, as much of the readily available, high-speed Internet pornography shows sex that is coercive, dehumanizing, and antirelationship. What we consume affects us, shaping how we experience ourselves, our desires, and our relationships. Stay in close contact with your gut as you consume erotic material, carefully tracking how you feel emotionally within your body. Erotic materials ought to enhance rather than replace intimate sex.

Be Flexible

Sexual desire ebbs and flows in an intimate relationship, and even very happy couples experience peaks and valleys in desire caused by everything from long work hours to the demands of parenting to age-related physical changes. There is no magic number for how often couples "should" have sex, and quality counts—not just quantity. Appreciate when sex is satisfying and bountiful, and be compassionate with yourself and your partner when it is not.

Although the partner whose desire is compromised can feel that he or she is to blame, low sexual desire in one or both partners is best viewed as a couples problem and addressed together as such. Low sexual desire that goes beyond normal relationship ebb and flow is a problem that tends not to resolve on its own, so be proactive and address it. Appendix 2 includes resources to help you find a therapist specifically trained to address sexual problems.

The Playground

Our cultural story is that sex ought to be easy. If we base our sexual expectations on the images and messages we see around us—the covers of magazines that promise three tricks for maximum pleasure or the steamy sex scenes we see in movies—we are at risk of feeling somehow wrong or deficient. We are at risk of feeling as though we don't measure up and judging ourselves harshly. In the real world, sex is complicated! Old stories can compromise our sex drive. Negative self-talk can block pleasure. Stress can make us feel downright unsexy. Plus, sex is created by two people together, so also in the mix are all of our partner's core issues and stories.

The erotic self is sneaky, subtle, and ever-changing, and the erotic self deserves attention and understanding. When partners are emotionally able to do what it takes to create self-aware sex, sex within an intimate relationship can feel like a *playground*—a safe and exciting space of self-expression that connects you to yourself, your partner, and all of life itself. When partners are unable to connect with themselves and each other, sex within an intimate relationship can feel a whole lot more like a *war zone*, fraught with all kinds of danger. Committing ourselves to self-awareness and self-compassion puts us on the path toward meeting each other on that playground, where sexual intimacy creates and sustains good feelings within and between partners. Whether a couple commits to sexual monogamy or creates another kind of sexual boundary that allows for sexual experiences with other people, the foundation of happy sex within an intimate relationship is self-awareness.

Sex is *developmental*. How you relate to sex at twenty is not the same as how you relate to sex at forty, and it's not the same as how you relate to sex at sixty. As you grow and change, what is possible for you sexually grows and changes as well. What remains true throughout your sexual journey is that your erotic self deserves the same brave exploration and illumination as all other aspects of your relational self. I believe that for all of us, the default setting is that the erotic self is a vital element of our humanity. "Stuff" gets in the way, for sure—traumatic experiences, cultural messages, and self-esteem and body image concerns can make it difficult to claim what is our birthright. Yet, the desire to touch and be touched, to give and receive pleasure, is universal.

Steps Toward Loving Bravely

Love is embodied—experienced within and expressed by your body. Knowing and embracing your erotic self fuels your intimate relationship.

Your Touch Story

Use the Name-Connect-Choose process to expand your awareness about your sexual self.

- **Name:** Reflect on your relationship with touch. In order to allow the right hemisphere of your brain to offer a variety of images and memories, begin this exercise in meditation. Sit quietly, close your eyes, and set an intention to explore your history with touch, especially affectionate touch. Journey through the chapters of your life: when you were with your family as a young child, when you were at school and with friends, when you were in your first few intimate relationships.

- **Connect:** As images and memories come up, notice what happens in your body: Comfort? Excitement? Fear? Warmth? Love? Be present with those feelings, allowing them to be exactly as they are. As you finish your meditation, jot down some notes about the meditation.

- **Choose:** How do those early images, stories, and experiences live within you today? What is the impact on you today? Which aspects of your touch story would you like to embrace and keep alive within you today? Which aspects would you like to release because they no longer serve you?

Sex Education

Reflect on how you learned about sex as you were growing up by answering the following questions:

How did your family educate you (or not) about sex?

How was sex talked about (or not) in your house?

What cultural stories about sex affect your relationship to your sexual self?

Are there religious and/or gendered messages about who you "should" be sexually that serve you well?

To what extent have you internalized messages about who you "should" be sexually that you would be better off without? How would you feel about your erotic self without those internalized messages?

Sexual Healing

Reflect on the most positive sexual experience that you have had in your life so far. Be specific in your mind about where you were, the person you were with, and what happened before, during, and after. Then write down some words and phrases in response to the following questions:

How did you feel within your body?

How did you feel about your partner?

What ingredients (setting, music, mood, and so forth) were in place that made the experience so great?

What could you do to carry the essence of that experience into future sexual experiences?

The Map of Your Body

Without deep awareness and understanding of how your body experiences sexual pleasure, your ability to experience sexual pleasure with another will likely be compromised. Make a list of your *erogenous zones*—the parts of your body or the areas of your body where you enjoy being touched—and the types of touch (light, deep, rhythmic) that feel good in those areas. Notice your gut reactions as you reflect on this.

If it was difficult to find much to say about how your body experiences pleasure, perhaps you would benefit from learning more about your erotic self. If you have never masturbated, or if you are very uncomfortable touching your own body, reflect on what that is about for you by completing the sentence: "Masturbation is...." Notice your gut reactions as you fill in that sentence.

Finally, respond to the following questions:

Is there a story (a cultural story, a family story, or a story that you created) that prevents you from exploring your own body?

Does that story constrain you in your sexual experiences with others?

If masturbation is framed as an avenue to self-understanding, self-acceptance, and self-love *in the service* of love with another, does this change your story at all?

Pornography and You

Complete this sentence: "Pornography is...." Reflect on your response. If you would like to explore this aspect of yourself more deeply, answer the following questions:

What is the impact of your use of pornography on your intimate relationships?

In what ways does pornography enhance you sexually? (For example, it helps you feel less self-conscious or increases your arousal.)

In what ways does it get in the way for you sexually? (For example, it makes you feel more self-conscious or makes your expectations rigid or unrealistic.)

Note: If you have only or mostly masturbated with pornography and/ or if you feel there's something problematic about your use of pornography (such as using frequently or using images that are violent, coercive, or disturbing), it is worth bravely addressing the impact pornography has on you.

Honor the Space Between

Sometimes, when we're lying together, I look at her and I feel dizzy with the realization that here is another distinct person from me, who has memories, origins, thoughts, feelings that are different from my own.

—Barack Obama

Whatever your politics, this quote is phenomenal. I have used it time and time again in my teaching because Barack Obama's words capture a vital aspect of love: honoring the space *between* self and other. In an intimate relationship, you are invited and challenged to hold on to yourself while connecting deeply with another person. In moments of peace, this is easy to do, but in moments of conflict and misunderstanding, this is no small task. But we must try to remember that love is a classroom. The space between self and other is a *crucible*, a container in which transformation occurs. *Your* words and actions shape *me*, and at the very same time *my* words and actions shape *you*.

The Thing About Conflict

The thing about conflict is that it's 100 percent inevitable. As my friend and colleague, Dr. Anthony Chambers, says, "The central task of any intimate relationship is the management of difference." Our experiences with our beloveds run the gamut from butterfliesin-my-stomach excitement to seeing-red angry. We simply can't have one without the other. Love is too rich and complex to allow us to pick and choose our emotions.

Building a life with someone is multifaceted. The same person you have mind-blowing sex with turns out to be the same person you share a bank account and a closet with. And that stuff can get really irritating! The best we can ever do is learn to deal lovingly with the frustrating and painful moments so that we can return as quickly as possible to a place of intimacy and friendship. Being truly brave means also trusting that conflict has within it the potential to *deepen* intimate connection by granting us the opportunity to know ourselves and our partner in a more vulnerable and authentic way. That's quite a dialectic: conflict sucks *and* conflict catalyzes growth. I don't know anybody who can hold that perspective all the time, but being able to catch glimpses of that both/and can make fighting more tolerable.

The story you tell yourself about conflict shapes your experience of it. The stories that people tell about conflict are so vital that every couples therapist addresses those stories in some way, shape, or form with every couple he or she sees, always. Regardless of how couples therapists are trained, one of the goals they will have for every couple they work with is to help the couple tell stories about their conflicts in a way that maximizes intimacy and minimizes blame and shame. **The goal is to move from linear conflict stories to systemic conflict stories.** But what exactly is the difference?

Linear Conflict Stories

When we tell a linear conflict story, we focus on cause and effect. "You did this to me." "I did this to you." Linear conflict stories tend to be simplistic and goal oriented, and the goal is usually to assign credit or blame: naming who the victim is, who had the worst behavior, whose fault it is. A linear conflict story is driven by all-or-nothing thinking, and the end result tends to be "zero sum," meaning that there is one so-called winner and one so-called loser. All of us are at risk of slipping into this kind of black-and-white storytelling, especially when we are upset. It's not altogether surprising. Our culture is full of examples of finger-pointing—from the endless tension between Democrats and Republicans to news stories that speak simplistically about victims and villains. We also are drawn to easy answers in an effort to conserve mental energy, as ambiguity and shades of gray simply require more work.

Telling a linear conflict story opens the door to a particular set of feelings, and that particular set of feelings tends to be relationally damaging:

"You did this to me" opens the door to anger and hurt.

"I did this to you" opens the door to shame.

Yes, we are responsible for our actions, always. *And*, blame and shame tend to be very corrosive elements in any relationship, including an intimate relationship. Let's look at clients of mine, Marius and Scarlett:

Marius came into my office furious with Scarlett. He said to her, "I cannot believe you went into my e-mail to find out if I sent my résumé to that job posting! How could you do this to me? You are nosy, and you betrayed my trust big-time." Marius's story is blaming (Scarlett betrayed his trust by searching his e-mail) and it goes in only one direction (Scarlett did something to him). This is an example of a linear conflict story.

Systemic Conflict Stories

On the other hand, when we tell a systemic story about the conflict in a relationship, the storyline is much more curvaceous. The narrative moves in a back-and-forth way, more a circle than a line. Declaring who started the fight is irrelevant because the storyteller bravely and humbly holds the awareness that both participate in the creation of this cyclical dance, and both feel hurt and misunderstood by the impact of it. Sidestepping the language of blame and shame, a systemic conflict story opts for keen observations about "the degree to which I do 'this' is the degree to which you do 'that.'" As Dr. Susan Johnson (2008) puts it: "The more I _____, the more you _____, and then the more I _____, and round and round we go" (88).

In a systemic conflict story, the storyteller keeps an eye on the space between self and other. The space between self and other is the *we*, and it is a third entity. The *we* requires a story thick enough and wide enough to hold the nuances of "my stuff," "your stuff," and "our stuff."

When we make the brave and difficult choice to stand in a systemic conflict story, we acknowledge that very little about intimate relationships is solvable anyway. A preeminent researcher and therapist, Dr. John Gottman, has found that a whopping 69 percent of the time, couples fight about a perpetual (rather than fixable) problem, so the goal is dialogue, not resolution (2011). Rather than simple fixing, most of the conflicts that a couple faces require *navigation*—skillfully and lovingly moving through in a way that minimizes damage.

Returning to the example of Marius and Scarlett, here's how it would sound if Marius had told a systemic conflict story: "I feel awful and embarrassed about my current unemployment, which leads me to withdraw and shut down, avoiding your questions. The more I shut down and withdraw, the more you feel alone and out in the cold. The more you feel abandoned by me, the more you pester me or resort to sneaky things like searching my e-mail in order to get information. The more you try to dig for information, the more I feel embarrassed and paralyzed, and round and round we go. We both play a part in this and we both feel awful about it."

Systemic conflict stories don't give you the primal satisfaction of destroying, triumphing, and conquering, but they help you avoid the pain of being crushed, obliterated, and victimized. Systemic conflict stories have breath and space, as they are told from a stance slightly above the fray—what Dr. Dan Wile, creator of Collaborative Couple Therapy (2002), calls a "second tier in the relationship, an observing post, a metalevel, a joint platform, an observing couple ego" (287). Systemic conflict stories transcend and transform.

Linear Conflict Stories	Systemic Conflict Stories
Zero sum (I win/you lose.)	What does the relationship need?
Cause and effect	Cycles/dances/circles
It's my fault/It's your fault.	The more I do "this," the more you do "that."
I can only see one next move.	I can see many possible next moves.
Shame or blame	Curiosity and sadness that we are fighting

The Marriage Hack

Northwestern University psychology professor Dr. Finkel and his colleagues (2013a) conducted a study that captures just how good systemic conflict stories are for an intimate relationship. Their so-called "marriage hack" experiment (2013b) involved recruiting 120 happy and recently married (for less than five years) couples. In the first year of the study, every four months, participants wrote about the most significant fight they had had in the previous four months.

In the second year of the study, the researchers divided the couples into two groups. The control group continued with the same plan (once every four months, they wrote about their most significant fight). The experimental group wrote a summary of their most significant fight as well, but in addition they wrote about the conflict from the perspective of a neutral third person who wants the best for both partners. They were asked to also include, if possible, a single positive aspect to the fight. The researchers wanted this second group to be able to keep this "outsider perspective" in mind all year long, so they also asked these couples to write about what might get in the way of them adopting this neutral third point of view during future fights and what they could do to keep that from happening. These additional writing prompts took each person in the second group about twenty-one extra minutes during the course of the year.

The results were amazing! Most studies about marriage unfortunately show that relationship satisfaction declines during the first year of marriage, and data from the couples in both groups showed that. But differences between the two groups emerged in the second year of the study. The couples in the control group, the ones who just wrote about their fights, continued to show declining levels of relationship satisfaction, whereas the couples in the second group, the ones who adopted the outsider perspective (a systemic conflict story), showed *no* additional decline and reported their fights were less distressing over time. Systemic conflict stories work!

Too Many Toothbrushes

My friend and mentor, Dr. Cheryl Rampage, has a great way of talking about how the shift from linear to systemic storytelling has helped her marriage. She says that early in her marriage, when she was in conflict with her husband, her story was about how much she couldn't stand *him*. Later, she became able to tell a story about how much she couldn't stand *this moment*. I have found this really helpful when I need to work with the story I am telling myself about the conflict in my marriage. Here's an example:

One evening, I sat in bed stewing. I had conjured up in my head a real doozy of a linear conflict story, and I was going to let Todd have it. I wasn't just angry, I was righteously angry. You know that kind of anger—the kind that makes you feel entitled and 100 percent sure you're right. I don't even know what triggered me—an unwashed dish or seeing him on his BlackBerry perhaps. What was in my head felt like a well-reasoned, logical argument outlining exactly how much I was doing around the house, how hard I was working, and how unappreciated I was. My story would show just how much he was wronging me.

He walked in, and I started up. My angry eruption put him on the defensive immediately. He managed to make some attempts to validate my emotions, to point out what he has been doing, and to remind me about the demands of his work life. Back and forth we went for a few minutes until our son, Brian, walked into the room. He had had a nightmare and wanted to sleep on the floor in our room. We made him a nest on the floor and headed into the bathroom to finish our argument.

The interruption had been enough of a jolt that I was beginning to view this fight a little differently. I was starting to see just how linear my conflict story was. It was simplistic, full of blame, and, worst of all, it was treating Todd as a threat that needed to be conquered rather than as the ally and friend I knew him to be. My righteous anger was starting to feel more like sadness. I also began to remember how unsolvable the problem really was. We were both busy. Life with two children was demanding, stressful, and tiring. We both were trying hard. Despite my initial cockiness that I had a new angle on an old problem, our fight was showing me that, in fact, this was a stale retread, and we were, as Dr. Dan Siegel calls it, "lost in a familiar place." I still loved this man, but I didn't love the moment we were in. I could see how the more I blamed him, the more he defended himself, and we were getting nowhere.

This shift toward a systemic conflict story was helping me, but what eluded me was how to make a graceful exit from this place neither of us wanted to be. My ego and pride were making it difficult to just express compassion for him, compassion for myself, and an apology for my harsh words and tone. So there we were, frustrated and confused, leaning against the sink, contemplating our next moves. Out of the corner of my eye, I noticed our toothbrush holder. Despite the fact that we are the only two people who use this bathroom, no fewer than eight toothbrushes were crammed into it.

Impulsively, I took the leap from frustration to curiosity, hoping that he would join me.

"Why the eff do we have so many toothbrushes?" We both smiled, and the tension began to melt. "Which one is yours?"

"The green one," he said.

"That can't be right," I said. "The green one is mine."

"I know," he said matter-of-factly. "You usually wake up earlier that I do, and I like yours because it's moist."

And scene. I was done! I broke into peals of laughter, surrendering myself to the never-ending paradox that is love. Nothing was solved that night. No answer was the final one. And I learned that, almost twenty years into a marriage, you can discover that there is a "marital toothbrush." No linear story can withstand this much nonsense, and through that fight, our relationship showed me, yet again, that the only possible story that can hold this degree of complexity is a systemic one.

Like all couples, Todd and I deserve gentleness, as we have valiantly attempted to work out a division of labor in order to meet the needs of our household—we need income, we need caretaking, we need to run the house, we need to be able to pursue our ambitions, we need to honor our individual passions, and we need time together. It will never be perfect, and it will never be done. I can advocate for my individual needs within the context of the "we," and so can he.

The degree to which I slip into a linear conflict story in which I am the victim and he is the villain is the degree to which he becomes defensive and shuts down. The degree to which I can extend compassion for myself, for him, and for our situation is the degree to which he can stay open and connected to me. A systemic conflict story invites us to sit shoulder-to-shoulder and look together at the challenges before us.

As spiritual teacher and bestselling author Neal Donald Walsh says, "My perspective creates my perception." Conflict is inevitable, but we have lots of choices in the face of conflict, including a choice of perspective. Because humans are emotional by nature, we will always be prone to slipping into a linear conflict story, but we can catch ourselves and course correct, reaching instead for a juicy systemic conflict story. From the perspective of a systemic conflict story, our perceptions change. Foe becomes ally. Conflict becomes a path back to compassion and curiosity…or at least humor and surrender.

Steps Toward Loving Bravely

Using a systemic (rather than linear) conflict story in the face of inevitable relationship problems is brave, helping you move through emotional pain and setting the stage for reconnection.

Blaming and Shaming

Your core issues (identified in lesson 2) likely dictate whether you tend more toward blame or shame, so let's figure out what kind of linear conflict stories (blame-filled or shame-filled) you tend to tell when you are upset. The "Guide for Moving from Reactivity to Intimacy" (http://www.newharbinger.com/35814) will remind you about the differences between linear and systemic conflict stories. In order to get clear about where your stories fall on the spectrum of blame-filled to shame-filled, do the following:

> Think about the last three fights or heated discussions or conflicts that you have been in. For each fight, write down what you were saying to yourself during the fight—for example, "I can't believe she's doing this to me" or "I screwed up so badly."

> Now, review your list. Does it seem as if you are more likely to slip into blame-filled linear conflict stories (all your partner's fault) or shame-filled linear conflict stories (all your fault) when you are upset? Perhaps you find yourself going back and forth between shame and blame?

> Is there a connection between your linear-conflict story and your core issue? For example, someone with a core issue related

to a fear of abandonment might slip into a shame-filled linear conflict story (such as "I am a screwup and he's going to leave me."). Someone with a core issue related to feeling constantly criticized might slip into a blame-filled conflict story (such as "She isn't listening to me and she's being unfair.").

Getting a better understanding of how you tend to talk to yourself when you are upset will help you in the next few lessons.

Love Hack

Whether or not you're currently in a relationship, try out Dr. Eli Finkel's "Marriage Hack" exercise.

Write about a recent fight you had with someone you care about from the perspective of a neutral third person who wants the best for all involved.

Next, write about how that neutral third person might find the good that could come from the fight.

Finally, write down what might make it difficult for you to adopt this neutral third-party point of view during a future fight.

Once you have written down your responses, reflect on how this exercise shifts your thoughts and feelings about the other person and about the fight.

Share the Love

Ask the person you had the fight with to complete the above exercise. Then, read each other's systemic conflict stories and talk together about what shifted for each of you through the writing. After talking with this person, reflect to yourself about how this dialogue felt different from the fight. What do you notice about a dialogue that is committed to a systemic conflict story rather than a linear one? What feels different? Is there less defensiveness and more curiosity?

Lesson 13

Respect the Pause

Between stimulus and response there is a space. In that space is our power to choose our response. In our response lies our growth and our freedom.

—Viktor Frankl

When a couple begins therapy, I ask, "What is it that is bringing you to therapy now?" Nine times out of ten the response I hear is, "We have a communication problem." This description doesn't really tell me much. It could mean that they yell and scream, or it could mean that they move through their home in stony silence for days on end. Author and couples therapist Dr. Anne Brennan Malec calls communication the oxygen in an intimate relationship (2015). It is the *how* of relational connection, captured in words, tone, and gestures. Communication problems, though real, are actually symptoms of much deeper issues at play.

By this point, you probably won't be surprised to know that what's most essential when it comes to healthy intimate communication is not some fancy set of skills. It's *relational self-awareness*— the ability and willingness to look honestly at what tends to set you off in your intimate relationship and how you handle yourself when you feel upset. When it comes to communication, relational self-awareness grows when we ask ourselves questions like:

How do I handle myself when there is conflict in my intimate relationship?

To what degree do I take responsibility for my part of the dance of communication?

What are the assets I bring to the table in times of turmoil?

What are my biggest stumbling blocks?

The High Road and the Low Road

The quote from Austrian psychiatrist and Holocaust survivor Viktor Frankl that opens this lesson captures an essential truth about communication—*there is always a space between stimulus and response.* Always. The *stimulus* is that thing out there that feels irritating, disappointing, or infuriating—the wet towel on the bathroom floor, the text message that seems awfully snippy, or the partner who saunters in thirty minutes late with no apology. The *response* is our reaction—what we do about that thing out there. We have zero control over the stimulus, but we have 100 percent control over the response.

This truth is simple in concept, but it is very difficult in practice. When someone does something that feels irritating, we tend to react quickly (think road rage). When that someone is our intimate partner, with whom the stakes are so high, our response can happen in the blink of an eye, and before we know it, we have done or said something that we will soon regret and that makes a situation go from bad to awful. It's hard work being human! We like to think of ourselves as evolved and sophisticated, yet those who dedicate their lives to the study of the human brain know that despite the brain's amazing complexity, we can shift from sophisticated to primitive pretty darn quickly.

The part of our brain called *the limbic system*, also known as *the emotional brain*, has been critical to the survival of our species. It is expert at making rough-and-dirty, instantaneous assessments of situations in order to keep us alive. It has basically two modes: fight or flight. When describing this part of the brain, therapist and researcher Dr. Dan Siegel uses this analogy: You are walking in the woods when, out of the corner of your eye, you see something that could be a stick or could be a snake. Your emotional brain makes a split-second assessment of possible danger, your body shifts into fight-or-flight mode, and you jump out of the way. Phew! Your emotional brain made a decision before you could assess possible responses, weigh pros and cons of each, and select a next step—a process that would have proven deadly had that object you saw been a snake. So thank goodness for the emotional brain.

Simple fight or flight is lifesaving in the deep woods, but it can be love-destroying in the family room. Responding in this rough-and-dirty way to our intimate partners, by either attacking (fight) or withdrawing (flight), doesn't promote closeness or safety. Fortunately, we have been blessed with a *cerebral cortex*, also known as the *new mammalian brain*, and it is quite sophisticated. One part of the cerebral cortex, *the prefrontal cortex*, is located right behind the center of the forehead, the area spiritual teachers call the "third eye." The prefrontal cortex, which is not fully wired up until we are twenty-five years old, can do a whole lot more than fight or flee. This part of the brain guides higher-order skills like empathy, compassion, wisdom, discernment, choice, and impulse control.

When we are processing the world through the prefrontal cortex, we are on the "high road." When we are processing the world through the limbic system, we are on the "low road." When faced with that infuriating stimulus, we are at risk of responding with our emotional brain in the blink of an eye, driving off the prefrontal cortex–guided high road and landing squarely on the limbic-guided low road, never even noticing the precious space between stimulus and response. The shift has happened. An openhearted, compassionate person becomes a warrior, just like that.

In Battle

Careening down the low road, at the mercy of your limbic system, you are in fight-or-flight mode, desperately trying to manage uncomfortable feelings of hurt, irritation, and/or anger. Your fight-or-flight behavior is your self-protective *survival strategy* (Sheinkman and Fishbane 2004)—behavior that is designed to manage painful emotions. Generally speaking, there are two kinds of survival strategies— *volume up* and *volume down* (Johnson 2008). When distressed, some of us resort to turning the volume up with fight-based survival strategies, and others of us resort to turning the volume down with flight-based survival strategies. Both kinds of survival tactics attempt to keep us safe—but with troubling consequences.

Fight: Volume-Up Survival Strategies

Those whose instinct is to stay and fight employ volume-up survival strategies, ones that involve getting *louder* or more extreme in response to feeling upset and threatened. Volume-up survival strategies include:

- Talking louder, more, and/or faster
- Yelling, "going off," or name-calling
- Threatening, giving consequences or ultimatums, retaliating, or seeking revenge
- Begging
- Blaming
- Repeating yourself
- Criticizing

In the extreme, volume-up strategies can include hitting (your partner, yourself, or something like a wall). When people yell as part of a volume-up strategy, in addition to their voice becoming louder, their words tend to become "bigger" and more severe ("you always" or "you never"). They may move from talking about this particular incident to talking about *all* the times they have felt disrespected, hurt, or betrayed in the relationship. Therapists sometimes call that *kitchen sinking*—bringing everything into the conversation, including the kitchen sink.

My client, Tess, has a black belt in volume-up survival strategies! One time, she and her boyfriend, Devon, were at a party, drinking, mingling, and dancing. They became separated at some point, and Tess couldn't find Devon anywhere. After looking for ten minutes, she found him—on the back porch talking with a very attractive woman. Tess approached Devon and told him it was time to go. As they walked home, Tess let Devon have it. "I cannot believe you. Who the hell was that? You are way out of bounds. How could you embarrass me like that?" And on and on. Her limbic system was in the driver's seat, and she had the volume turned way up.

Flight: Volume-down Survival Strategies

In contrast, volume-down survival strategies involve getting *quieter* in order to cope with feeling triggered and include:

- Shutting down or withdrawing

- Walking away

- Giving the silent treatment

- Not answering phone calls, texts, e-mails, and the like

- Sulking

- Pouting

- Relying on nonverbal communication: slamming doors, huffing and puffing, rolling your eyes, crossing your arms

Volume-down strategies are a different way of taking yourself out of a painful moment. Perhaps you withdraw because you are hurting too badly to stay present in the face of so much pain. Perhaps you withdraw in order to hurt the other person. Your behavior communicates, "I don't know how to tell you about my pain with words, so I will show you with my actions."

Note that removing yourself from a painful situation in order to calm down and decide how you want to proceed is *not* the same as using a volume-down self-protective survival strategy. This helpful strategy is called *pressing pause*. More on that later.

Return for a moment to the example of Tess and Devon and imagine that rather than being prone to volume-up survival strategies, Tess is prone to volume-down survival strategies. Here's how the walk home may have looked: As they walked, Devon reached for Tess's hand but Tess pulled away. Devon asked Tess what was wrong, and Tess mumbled, "I'm fine. Just tired." When they got home, Tess remained quiet, put on her PJs, and got in bed without saying good-night.

History Repeats Itself

Our survival strategies tend to arise within our family context. The early classroom of the family shows us so much about how to handle the inevitable differences that emerge when lives entwine in love. Stimulus. Space. Response. Self-awareness grows when we ask ourselves questions like:

What did the people who raised me show me about the space between stimulus and response?

How did the adults in my life manage their feelings of upset, irritation, and anger?

What sorts of low-road behaviors were most common in my house growing up?

Some of us use self-protective survival strategies that *mirror* what we saw growing up. For others, memories of a parent who was prone to fits of rage, for example, create an urge to behave in exactly the *opposite* way, out of fear of *becoming* that parent. The desire to break the legacy is noble; however, turning 180 degrees is rarely the best option. In this case, 180 degrees from raging requires shutting down and disengaging from self and other. The consequence of tamping down emotions is steep and likely creates disconnection from self, loss of vitality, and emotional numbness. While it is certainly understandable to never want to become what you feared as a child, commit yourself to finding a shade of gray between rage and suppression. The work we are doing here will support your process.

Embracing a brave and deep way of loving yourself and others requires curiosity about what else is possible. Growing beyond fighting or fleeing takes guts. Motivation to change sometimes can be found by recalling how your parents' use of survival strategies felt to you as a kid. Helping my clients remember how lonely they felt when their mom disappeared into her room in obvious but unspoken pain, or how frightened they felt when their dad yelled, can provide powerful motivation to claim healthier ways to handle big feelings. The key question is this: what would have been different for you if that parent had learned to honor the space between stimulus (whatever upset him or her) and response (yelling or hiding)?

Pressing Pause

When something happens and emotions come rushing in, you are at a fork in the road with multiple possibilities ahead. The first step, and it's a huge step, is *pressing pause*. Pressing pause gives you the chance to remember that something beyond fighting or fleeing exists. Pausing is an adaptive *time-out* that allows you to claim some stillness and some time. When you pause, you commit yourself to not talking, texting, calling, or otherwise acting…yet. In your pause, you may choose to go into a separate space, especially if you and your partner were in the same room when the incident occurred. Here are some ideas to keep in mind:

- **Verbalize the need for a pause.** Say something like, "I'm really upset, and I'm taking a pause" or "I need to go calm down for a little while. I can't talk right now." Saying this out loud instead of just walking away is especially helpful if you tend toward a volume-down survival strategy like withdrawing and shutting down, because pressing pause is *not* the same thing as withdrawing. It is step one on a journey toward compassion for yourself and the other person.

- **Use "I" or "we" statements.** Some partners make an agreement that either of them is authorized to call a *time-out* when they feel flooded or upset. It is best to say, "*I* need a time out" or "I think *we* need a time out," instead of saying, "*You* need a time out," which takes your attention away from your own experience and invites the other person's defensiveness.

- **Consider creating a safety word.** Because it can be hard to choose careful and thoughtful language when upset, some couples come up with a *safety word* that communicates to the other person that some time and a space to calm down is needed. It doesn't matter what the word is (cantaloupe... armadillo). What matters is that you and your partner know that the safe word indicates a break in the action. It is a way of saying, "I'm a mess. This is a mess. I need space."

- **Practice mindful breathing.** As you will practice in the exercises at the end of this lesson, when you pause, it can be helpful to take some deep breaths. Place one hand on your heart and one hand on your belly. Bring your attention to your breathing, noticing your inhale and your exhale. This mindfulness strategy brings your attention to the present moment and changes your physiology. Think of the deep breaths as opening a door to your different, consciously chosen, self-aware, and brave response.

If we all committed ourselves to pressing pause, the world would be a very different place. Reality shows would have to reinvent themselves. Viewers watch *The Real Housewives of* _____ because volume-up self-protective survival strategies, while awful for intimate relationships, apparently make for great TV. Much of the suffering that happens in relationships, intimate and otherwise, changes and dissolves when we press pause.

Committing yourself to just this first step is huge, and when you are able to do it, I invite you to celebrate! Growing your ability to notice you are upset and pause before responding is hard and brave work for a number of reasons. First, the stuff that sets you off is likely related to your core issues, meaning it's old and deep. Second, taking a pause requires you to win a battle over your biology. Your emotional brain is much "older" in an evolutionary sense than your wise, flexible prefrontal cortex, so taking a pause requires a newer and more fragile part of your brain to conquer an ancient warrior. Third, woven into the very nature of feeling upset and reactive is a sort of entitlement and arrogance. When upset, we tend to believe that the situation *demands* an immediate response and that our first response is, in fact, the best response. Lastly, we live in a world that moves at lightning speed, so it makes sense that we tend to think that a fast response is a better response. Saying that someone can really "think on her feet" is a compliment. I think that we should instead value the ability to say, "This is important, so I want to take some time before I respond."

Volume-up survival strategies can seem so compelling because the situation before us feels out of control, and therefore we feel out of control. We are uncomfortable, so we want to act on our environment—to do something that makes us feel "in control" again. But taking a pause opens up the possibility that, rather than being a victim of our reactivity and our environment, we can claim some *real power*—power over ourselves, power to choose how we want to respond (Fishbane 2013). Taking a pause is the true way to gain control. In the next lesson, we will talk about *how* you can choose to respond once you have gained the power of choice.

Standing at a Crossroads: Reactive Breakups

Before ending this lesson, I want to include a thought about *reactive breakups*. Breaking up with your partner in the midst of a painful, awful conflict is the outer edge of a volume-down self-protective survival strategy. If the pain feels too great, ending the relationship may seem like the only way to stop the hurt. However, discernment is warranted. Reactive breakups that happen in the throes of a fight-or-flight response carry hidden risks. Even as you are attempting to stop the pain, you may create additional pain. Calling it quits as a means of self-protection may make you more likely to reengage in the relationship once the strong feelings have passed, allowing the same old conflict pattern to continue: break up, make up, fight, retreat, repair, reinjure. This dance is exhausting for everyone involved. The dance perpetuates disconnection from oneself, and the dance erodes trust between partners.

Reactive flight-based breakups also tend to kick up so much dust that the deeper self-learning is lost. As the saying goes, "You bring yourself with you." This means there is risk of repeating this same pattern in your next relationship. If and when old drama replays in a new relationship, you certainly deserve compassion, and the opportunity for learning and healing is always there. However, because self-awareness changes old patterns, it is empowering to say, "I will no longer hide from myself. Love is a classroom, and I want to access the learning housed within my pain." It takes great courage to dive into the pain that hides beneath flight, to hold awareness for the old stories that fuel the urge to run away. Those old stories may be quite tender: *I am worthless... I am incapable of loving someone... I am damaged beyond repair.* These old stories, like desperately sad children, need compassion and tender loving care.

The decision to stay or leave is separate and apart from the quiet internal work of honoring the pain beneath your self-protective behavior. Although running may provide relief in the moment, if you can stay present with the pain beneath the urge to flee, you are more likely to ultimately make a choice that is *empowered* instead of *reactive.* To grow like this, you must trust that no matter what the other person is doing, saying, or being, it is always of great value to look at the aspect of yourself that is being emotionally stirred. **Study your reactivity.** What is the old story about yourself that needs to be brought into the light of love? From this quiet place of deep friendship with yourself, the decision to stay or go changes. Rather than a need to hang on, to escape, or to punish the other person, you can make an empowered choice based on the value of this relationship in your life.

Steps Toward Loving Bravely

When upset, we are prone to sprinting past the precious and precarious space between stimulus and response, yet freedom blossoms when we take ourselves into our own power.

Volume Up and Volume Down

Look back at the lists of survival strategies (in the section "In Battle"). Write down the specific ones you tend to use when you are upset. (Alternatively, download the list from http://www.newharbin ger.com/35814 and circle the responses you commonly have.) When you become reactive to someone else's words or behaviors (the stimulus), are you prone to fighting or fleeing (response)?

Take note of how you feel as you work on naming your patterns. If you feel defensive or judgmental, try to shift into a place of compassionate curiosity, knowing that, as you do, you are sowing the seeds of transformation.

The Apple and the Tree

Now refer to the same list of behaviors and, with different colored pens, write down or circle the survival strategies used by the adults in your family of origin. Reflect on the overlaps and the differences. How are *your* fight-or-flight behaviors similar to or different from the ones you saw the grown-ups in your home use when you were growing up? To what extent did your parents' conflict style create the roots of your self-protective survival strategies?

Pressing Pause

Commit to the practice of pressing pause when you feel yourself starting to shift from calm and open to fight-or-flight mode. Try the ideas below and see what works best for you. (The "Guide for Moving from Reactivity to Intimacy" at http://www.newharbinger.com/35814 has a list you can keep handy when you need to strategize a helpful response).

- **Belly breathing:** Put your hand on your belly, just below your ribs. As you inhale through your nose, push your belly out against your hand. Exhale slowly through your mouth. Repeat three to ten times and notice what changes within you.

- **Count to ten:** Before you say or do anything, slowly count to ten. Notice what changes within you.

- **Mindful break:** Before you say or do anything, take a mindful break. Bring your attention to the present moment without judgment. Simply describe what each of your five senses is experiencing right here, right now. What are you seeing, hearing, smelling, touching, and tasting?

- **Sensory input:** Some people find it helpful to enhance a mindful break by seeking intense sensory input. See whether adding sensory input enhances your ability to sit in the pause using one of these examples:
  - Suck on a mint.
  - Rub your hand against something comforting like fleece.
  - Smell something good like a candle or soap.
  - Listen to music.

- **Love altar:** Create a love altar by arranging special photos and mementos in a sacred place in your home. This does not have to be elaborate! Supercharge any of the above "Pressing Pause" practices by doing them while sitting at your altar. A love altar can help you stay connected to why these emotion-regulation practices are so important.

Lesson 14

Dig a Little Deeper

As lovers, we poise together delicately on a tightrope... To stay on the rope, we must shift with each other's moves, respond to each other's emotions.

—Sue Johnson

In the face of inevitable conflict, we are at risk of giving in to a reactive desire to fight or flee, yet our bravest moves are those that shift us from *reactivity* to *intimacy*. But how? The previous lesson ended with an invitation to practice inhabiting the pause, the precious and precarious space between stimulus and response, where Viktor Frankl finds our human freedom. Within that pause are an array of possibilities that go far beyond the black-and-white nature of the fight-or-flight response. When you take the risk to dig a little deeper, what you access is your *vulnerability*—your most authentic expression of self—thereby creating the potential to deepen the connection with yourself and with your intimate partner.

Emotional Reactivity

Spoiler alert: no matter how hard we try, we will never fix or cure our emotional reactivity. That's not even a healthy aspiration, as our emotions, even the messy ones, make us who we are. Our emotional life is a critical part of being human. Experiences of sadness, fear, anger, happiness, and surprise color the stories of our lives, and though we may prefer to experience only the so-called "positive" emotions, the so-called "negative" emotions are just as real and valuable. Emotions are the natural response to life, and we are most able to connect with others when we can stay present with our feelings.

Knowing we will never stop having emotional reactions to the world around us, or to our partner specifically, we can set two goals for ourselves:

> To reduce the amount of time it takes to notice that we have exited the high road and are barreling ahead on the low road (to catch ourselves in fight-or-flight mode)

> To be courageous enough to move away from our self-protective fight-or-flight survival strategies and to speak instead from a vulnerable place that is braver and deeper

From Reactivity to Vulnerability

The imperfect journey of shifting from reactivity to vulnerability involves a process:

1. Your partner has done something (stimulus).

2. You feel something (response).

3. You press pause so that you can study your reactivity.

4. You use the Name-Connect-Choose process to help you move from intimacy-preventing reactivity to intimacy-inviting vulnerability.

The first three parts were covered in the previous lesson. This lesson will teach you how to do the last part.

Name: Tell Yourself the Story

When we get upset, everything inside starts to feel very messy very quickly. Fragmented thoughts swirl, emotions swell, and our bodies become distraught. By pressing pause, you lessen the impact of these reactions and can more easily move on to this next step.

Start by simply *describing* to yourself what has happened. You can tell the story inside your head or you can write it down. Make sure you back up and start with the events that *led up to* your upset feelings so that you can look at the context of the upsetting moment itself. Start with the big picture and then narrow it down to the specifics of what happened. Naming the sequence of events in this way does two things at once:

> It provides you with some internal organization, helping you feel less confused and calmer.

> It can help you see something you didn't see before, shifting you from a *linear conflict story* to a *systemic conflict story.*

Remember Tess, who got really upset when she saw her boyfriend, Devon, talking with the beautiful stranger? Let's imagine what might happen if, instead of launching into fight-or-flight mode, she had been able to pause and then use the Name-Connect-Choose process to shift herself from reactivity to vulnerability. Here's how that might have looked:

Devon finds Tess outside the party, and he can tell that she's upset. He asks what's wrong, and she says, "I'll tell you at some point, but I need some time to calm down and figure some stuff out first." As they walk home, she does some "press pause" work. She takes deep breaths of the crisp night air. She feels her feet on the earth. She listens attentively, silently naming the various sounds around her, trusting that doing these sensory, present-moment acts will create shifts in her. Her feelings are huge right now, her thoughts are all over the place, and her body is on edge. Inside her head, she is talking to herself the way a parent might talk to an upset child, telling herself that these feelings make sense and that this painful moment won't last forever. Part of her desperately wants to give in to her emotional reactivity and make it all about Devon, but another part of her knows that love is a classroom. This wise part of her trusts that this moment contains hidden gems, and that her relationship with herself and with Devon will benefit from her journey within.

She begins to tell herself the story of what happened that evening, hoping that naming her experience will help her start to feel at least a little curious. She reflects on the beginning of the party. She and Devon were talking among their friends. As Tess was telling a story about her boss, she glanced over at Devon and noticed that he was checking his phone. She recalls that she felt annoyed but said nothing to him about it. Later, Tess went to the bathroom. On her way out, she caught a glimpse of herself in the mirror and thought, "Ugh, why did I wear this dress?! I look so frumpy!" Shortly after that, she saw Devon talking with the mystery woman. Tess notes that she had felt disappointed and embarrassed seeing Devon checking his phone. She also notes that the negative assessment she made of herself in the bathroom further shifted her mood, making her feel less bubbly, less chatty, and vaguely sad. She felt upset about her appearance, but also upset that she was being so hard on herself about her appearance. Seeing Devon talking to that woman now seems like maybe it was the last straw.

In telling herself the story of the evening, Tess's awareness expands as she notes two new "data points." Her initial, emotionally flooded story was, "Devon is a jerk. I knew eventually he would do this to me. I was a fool for trusting him." Now that she has paused and told herself a more detailed and contextual story of the evening, she wonders, "To what degree is my anger at Devon shaped by the fact that I felt hurt that he was distracted during my work story and by the fact that I was being mean to myself? If I had seen myself in the mirror and said, 'Damn, girl, looking good,' how would I have reacted to Devon's behavior? Perhaps I would have just walked over and joined the conversation."

She has no answers, but in pausing and telling herself the story of the evening, she has shifted from a thin and linear black-and-white conflict story ("Devon is a jerk") to a thick and systemic dialectical (both/and) conflict story: "Devon and I were having fun. *And* I felt a little hurt and confused by his behavior. *And* I felt quite self-critical. *And* I felt really upset that he was talking to that woman."

Connect: Find the Feeling Behind the Feeling

Telling yourself the story of what has happened can help you begin to identify and connect with your feelings. And there is usually more than one feeling swirling inside. Dr. Sue Johnson makes a helpful distinction between *secondary* and *primary* feelings. *Secondary feelings* accompany and fuel the self-protective survival strategies that are running the show when we are in fight-or-flight mode: anger, outrage, and irritation. Secondary feelings are like a coat of armor, making us feel that we are safe and nobody can hurt us.

Anger is the most common secondary emotion and warrants special attention. As with any of our emotions, there's nothing bad or wrong with anger. Anger just is. Anger can alert us that a boundary has been violated. Anger can be a call to action. Anger can wake us from an emotional slumber. But anger requires our "A game." Anger is rarely helpful when expressed in its raw form. It insists that we work bravely with it, transforming coal to diamond. We must honor anger as a valuable signal emerging from within, while at the same time recognizing that in order to use our anger for good, we must *engage* it rather than allowing it to run the show. Engaging our anger means working skillfully and respectfully with it, as you will learn to do in this lesson. When we do this, we validate ourselves and respect the other person, accelerating emotional growth and promoting healing.

You see, there is usually something else going on, something hiding out beneath and behind the anger. That something is a *primary feeling*—the feeling behind the feeling. Primary feelings are more vulnerable, more tender, and softer than secondary feelings. They include sadness, shame, loneliness, fear, and inadequacy. There is a huge payoff, internally and relationally, for honoring our primary feelings.

But it's hard. Many of us would do just about anything to avoid primary feelings. Men especially are taught to avoid them like the plague—don't feel them and, if you do, certainly don't share them. Men and women alike have been conditioned to believe that primary feelings indicate weakness and that exposing them would make their partners turn and run. In couples therapy, when I am able to help a partner shift from expressing secondary feelings to expressing primary feelings—from anger to sadness, for example—the payoff is amazing! Invariably, the other person softens, leans in, and affirms that there is great strength in vulnerability (Brown 2015).

When you are in the throes of a secondary feeling, such as anger, *connect* with the feeling behind the feeling. **Remember that behind an angry person is a hurt person.** Take the risk to compassionately connect with your hurt (your primary feelings) without judgments about whether you "should" feel hurt. As you begin to connect with a primary feeling, simply welcome it, stay present to it, and feel it. Feelings simply are, so questioning their validity is a road to nowhere.

Back to Tess. The pause she took calmed her body down. Naming the story of the evening helped her feel less confused and more open to possibilities beyond her reactive, linear story that "Devon is a jerk." She still feels angry, but now she is also connecting with primary feelings behind her anger. The image that comes into her mind is that the secondary feeling—the anger—is a jar of navy blue paint. The primary feelings that are rising to her awareness— fear and shame—are white paint, being mixed into the navy blue. The blue color is still there, but it is changing. She holds awareness of her fear. Her fear is saying that if Devon is talking to another woman, he will leave her for someone else. She holds awareness of her shame. Her shame is saying that Devon's apparent interest in another woman means that she is not enough for him. She starts to cry. She is bravely letting herself feel these primary emotions. Part of her is saying, "This is hard! It's much easier just to focus on how wrong he is." And another part of her feels proud that she is handling herself this way.

Choose: Give Voice to Primary Feelings

After naming and connecting, it is time to choose your response. Choose a response that is guided by a question Neal Donald Walsh encourages us to ask: "What would love do?" From this hard-earned place of choice, as you hold awareness of your story and your pain, you have the opportunity to *do* what love would do. Love speaks truth in the service of intimate connection. Love speaks the language of primary feelings. Love speaks vulnerably: "I am hurting so badly… I am desperate to be seen and heard… I am questioning my worth… I feel unsteady and unsure… I could use some comfort." When you choose to give voice to your primary feelings, you increase your chances of authentic engagement and care from your partner— even if he or she is also hurting. Rage and defensiveness cannot persist in the face of authentic vulnerability. *Your* ability to choose love transforms the entire relationship dance.

Sometimes when you give voice to your primary feelings, that's the end of it. Apologies are offered and forgiveness is granted. We let go and move on. Other times, vulnerably giving voice to primary feelings is an invitation to dive even deeper. When you shift into voicing primary feelings, curiosity flourishes, and now, as students in the same classroom, you can look *together* at whether and how the past is shaping the present moment. Are old stories in the room, adding confusion to the present moment, as they are prone to do? Safer in the presence of your partner, you can explore:

What does this feeling I have right now remind me of from my past?

When was the first time I felt this way?

Who from my past related to me the way my partner is relating to me now?

Sharing at this level creates deeper knowledge of yourself and your partner. It grows trust by allowing your partner to see you in your fullness and to love you anyway. This kind of sharing also offers healing to the wounded kid who lives inside of you and who still carries the old story. In the light of love, the wounded child's burden is lessened.

Now let's return to Tess and Devon: Tess wipes her eyes and takes a deep breath. She's not quite able to look at Devon as she speaks, but she begins to open up to him about her tender feelings. Devon listens. His quiet presence invites her to dig even deeper. She talks with Devon about her parents' divorce. As an adult, Tess can hold a complex story about the multiple factors that led to the divorce, and, as an adult, Tess knows that the divorce was not her fault. But the wounded child within Tess recalls her dad's heartbreak when he found out about her mom's affair, and her old story is that "Mom cheated on *us*." The wounded girl is terrified that she will never be "enough" to make someone stay. As Tess gives voice to that old shame-loaded story, Devon neither diminishes her nor recoils from her. He holds a steady, compassionate place for the story of her wounded child.

Being in love with Devon puts Tess face-to-face with her old stories. There's no way around it. Ultimately, she cannot control whether Devon stays or goes. Nor can he control whether *she* stays or goes. But by working with her emotional reactivity—consequently her vulnerability—she bravely transforms conflict into connection, allowing her and Devon to move through this moment in a way that doesn't do damage to their relationship and instead brings them closer together.

Because communication is the oxygen of an intimate relationship, care and attention to all that is within and between us ensures healthy air quality. We become reactive precisely because the relationship matters so much. Love *demands* that we become students of our reactivity, seeking rich understanding not only of the nature of our emotional reactivity and the survival strategies we employ in the face of strong emotions, but also of the wisdom and beauty that swirl behind our pained facades.

Steps Toward Loving Bravely

Digging a little deeper means telling the story of your upset (name), exploring the feelings behind the feelings (connect), and giving voice to your vulnerability (choose) in order to authentically connect with yourself and your partner.

From Reactivity to Intimacy

Our Name-Connect-Choose process will help you dig a little deeper in order to shift from reactivity to intimacy. The next time you find yourself getting upset with someone you are close to, pause and then take yourself through these steps. The online "Guide for Moving from Reactivity to Intimacy" summarizes these steps (http://www.newharbinger.com/35814).

1. **Name: Tell yourself the story.** Start by telling yourself the story of what happened. Make sure you "rewind" inside your head to the events that preceded your upset feeling. Think about all the details surrounding what occurred, not just the moment you became upset.

2. **Connect: Find the feeling behind the feeling.** Allow yourself to be present with your emotions. What do you notice? Where in your body do you feel it? What does it feel like? If you can only access secondary feelings like anger, keep breathing with the anger, thinking about what message it carries. What does the anger need you to know? What are its demands? Stay curious about what else might be there, hiding quietly behind the anger. As you become aware of other feelings, particularly primary feelings, welcome them and listen to them without judgment. Your curiosity holds healing power.

3. **Choose: Give voice to primary feelings.** It's time! Step boldly into voice, trusting that there is great strength in your vulnerability. Talk with your loved one about your primary feelings. I

hope that your brave choice is met with a compassionate and caring response. If you are met with anything less than compassion and care, remember that the other person's response belongs to him or her and says nothing about you. It does, however, give you data—about the amount of safety within the relationship and about the nature of the other person's woundedness.

Build the Cushion

While healthy adults are able to self-regulate and self-soothe when upset, we don't outgrow our need for soothing and regulation from others, especially intimate others.

—Mona DeKoven Fishbane

In an intimate relationship, there is an overriding ultimate equation for success: ***Do less of the bad and do more of the good.*** Do less of the stuff that creates disengagement, distance, and resentment and do more of the stuff that creates closeness, trust, and empathy. The choices we make when facing difficult moments with those we love powerfully shape the course of events. In this lesson we will explore practices that help us do more of the good in our intimate relationship, because actively working to build the cushion of positive connection reduces the chances of slipping into hostility and suffering. We will talk about two practices, both of which begin *within* and have impact *between*: making mindful language choices and embracing love languages.

Seven Traps and Seven Reaches

Although the escalated language of fight and the icy silence of flight are obvious, there are some subtle language choices that we make in our intimate relationships that aren't as clear-cut but that still send us down a slippery slope. Let's look at seven common but problematic relational language choices, or *intimacy-preventing traps.* For each of these seven intimacy-preventing traps, I am offering an alternative—an *intimacy-inviting* reach. These are language choices that support a brave shift toward vulnerability and authenticity, allowing us to reach across the space between self and other with an invitation to connect. It is amazing how subtle or small shifts in language affect how you perceive and experience the moment with your partner and consequently profoundly shape how your partner experiences you. Committing yourself to speaking from the *intimacy-inviting reaches* goes a long way toward building a cushion of relational positivity that's good for everyone.

1. Trap: "You Need To..."

On the low road, things—you, your partner, the world—feel very out of control, and you may begin talking to your partner like this: "You need to _____ [apologize to me...take responsibility for your actions...call your brother...stop spending so much money]." This is the language of control, and it is guided by the fear-based belief that if the other person changes, you'll feel better. Even if this happens to be accurate, this language is intimacy-preventing because we tend to mount resistance in the face of another's effort to control us, and a battle of wills ensues. Does this sound familiar? "You need to send that e-mail." "No I don't!" "Yes you do!"

Reach: "I Feel So..."

When you feel out of control like this, rather than saying, "You need to...," see what happens when you begin to see the urge to control your external world and the people in it as a cue to you that something must feel awful inside of *you.* Instead of trying to control others, tune in to that awful feeling and give it voice. For example, instead of saying, "You need to get a job," try saying "I feel so scared about money. You have been out of work for six months, and the bills are piling up. I am terrified, and I feel as if my concerns are being ignored." This is the brave language of vulnerability. Letting your partner into your world invites empathy, collaboration, and closeness.

2. Trap: "You Make Me Feel..."

When we are upset in the face of another's actions or inactions, it is so easy to move into blame, saying, "You make me feel so _____ [awful, ugly, worthless, stupid, angry, exhausted]." This kind of statement is intimacy-preventing for three reasons. First, this language implies *intent* that may or may not be there. The *impact* of your partner's actions may be that you feel awful without your partner intending for you to feel that way. Be careful not to travel too deeply into another's head! Second, this language is the essence of abandoning yourself. In this language, you have given away your power and put yourself at the mercy of another. When you abandon yourself, there can be no intimacy with another person. Third, this language reflects that you have forgotten about that precious and precarious space between stimulus and response. Your partner acted in a certain way (stimulus). There is a space. You feel awful (response). What else, besides a thin story of intentional hurt and blame, is possible in that powerful space between stimulus and response?

Reach: XYZ Statement

When upset, I love the suggestion from Drs. Howard Markman and Scott Stanley (2010) to use an XYZ statement. An XYZ statement goes like this: "When you do X, in situation Y, I feel Z." For example, "When you roll your eyes as I'm talking about the fight I had with my brother, I feel angry, invalidated, and unimportant." The difference is subtle yet powerful. In an XYZ statement, you are doing three intimacy-inviting things at once: holding the other person accountable for his or her actions (but not for your feelings), giving context, and taking responsibility for your feelings. This brave reach changes everything—within you and between you and your partner.

3. Trap: The Disembodied "You"

During a therapy session, Mary explained a struggle she was having in her intimate relationship. She said, "You just don't know whether you should stay or go. You feel like he's a good guy but you feel scared." I invited her to shift her language. "Mary, what you're saying is so important, but I'd really like you to say it again, this time using 'I' instead of 'you.'" Mary looked puzzled but agreed: "I just don't know whether I should stay or go. I feel like he's a good guy but I feel scared." As Mary shifted her language, her face softened and tears filled her eyes. When I train new therapists, I urge them to listen vigilantly for this subtle yet meaningful language choice, and I urge them to invite their clients to shift from the disembodied "you." It is much more than just a minor detail or semantic concern. It's about how you stand vis-à-vis your story.

Reach: The embodied "I"

The alternative to the disembodied "you" is to commit to saying "I" when talking about yourself. When you do this, you engage your story as deeply and uniquely yours and insist on connection to yourself, knowing it is the precursor for connection with another person. When you catch yourself slipping into the disembodied "you," ask yourself what is going on. Is the disembodied "you" an attempt to avoid your pain? What if you invited your pain in, held it as you would a distressed child, and trusted your resilience?

4. Trap: "Why Did You...?"

Asking "Why did you...?" or "Why didn't you...?" invites defensiveness.

Reach: "What Kept You From...?"

Asking "What kept you from...?" invites collaboration. If you ask your partner, "Why did you lie to me?" you invite him or her to explain the cause of his or her behavior to you. In all likelihood, your partner's voice will sound and feel defensive to you, the story he or she tells isn't going to feel satisfying to you, and the pain of the lie will remain. Instead, try asking your partner a *constraint question* (Pinsof et al. 2015): "What kept you from being truthful with me?"

A constraint question orients you and your partner toward the behavior you desire: truth. It invites your partner to talk with you about what gets in the way of truth, putting you both on a path toward a systemic conflict story. Your partner's answer may be: "What kept me from telling you the truth is my fear of your reaction." The story has just gone from *linear* ("you lied to me") to *systemic* ("something is keeping you from being honest with me").

What is your stuff? What is my stuff? What is our stuff? That becomes the work! The possibility for side-by-side collaboration emerges. Your pain in the wake of the lie (or other behavior) remains valuable, because it invites you both to mine together for the complex truths that exist within and between you.

5. Trap: Should or Shouldn't

Musterbation is the desire for a set of rules for how things should be. Dr. Albert Ellis coined this term to capture our tendency to argue with our present reality as it exists right here, right now. Usually musterbation appears in our relationships in the form of a "should." For example, "You should plan a night out for us. That's what people do for each other." Similar to "you need to," the language of "should" reflects a quest for control and a difficulty remembering that all we can ever control is ourselves. Slipping into the language of should and shouldn't creates a barrier between you and your partner. It also creates a barrier between you and happiness!

Reach: Give Voice to What You Want

Use your "should" language as a signal to yourself that an unmet need or longing within you is desperate for attention. Give voice to that instead. Far more vulnerable and therefore intimacy-inviting, asking for what you need soothes you and changes the course of the conflict. "I am longing for…" "I am desperate for…" "I would love for you to…" "It would mean a lot to me if you would…" For example, instead of using a "should" statement, see what happens if you say: "I would love for you to plan a night out for us. I am really longing for some time together, and it would mean a lot to me if you took the lead on it."

6. Trap: Always or Never

In the face of conflict, it is easy to become polarized, reflected by use of words like "always" and "never." Insisting that your partner always or never does something or says something probably isn't accurate. And even if it happens to be accurate, it is another invitation for defensiveness. In the face of your "always" or "never," your partner will probably do one of two things:

Try to think of an exception to your declaration

Try to recall something that *you* always or never do

The linear back-and-forth blame game will continue, and you'll end up feeling farther apart.

Reach: Often, Lately, Rarely, It Seems

Recognize that "always" and "never" language is usually an effort to turn the volume up in order to be heard. You need to be heard, and you deserve to be heard. But if you find yourself slipping into "always" or "never" language, try softening to "often," "lately," or "rarely." Another option is to remember that perspective shapes perception; frame your observation as coming from your point of view by saying, "It seems to me that…" or "It feels to me like…" This intimacy-inviting shift lets your partner know that even as you're feeling hurt and confused, part of you knows there's more to the story than what you can see right now.

7. Trap: How Can I Get My Partner to...?

This final intimacy-preventing trap is one that is likely said inside your head or over a glass of wine with a friend. And it's sneaky. Saying "How can I get him to..." is problematic. Voicing your concern in this way indicates that you believe that you do not have authentic power and that you must resort to *indirect means* of getting what you want. If this is your perception, use it as a warning sign that something is amiss within your relationship because in a healthy intimate relationship, wants and needs are legitimized, validated, and given space. Whether, how, and when the want or need gets met is a separate matter, but in a healthy intimate relationship each partner is able to verbalize his or her longings.

Reach: Label What You Really Want or Need

The antidote to this trap is the Name-Connect-Choose process. *Name* your longing or your unmet need, *connect* with the vulnerable feelings attached to the unmet need, and *choose* to directly ask for what you want. Here's an example.

- Name: I long for more touch in our relationship.

- Connect: I feel sad and unimportant.

- Choose: I am going to bring this up as a problem.

It may also be helpful to let your partner know that you are stuck in this intimacy-preventing trap. This way the two of you can wonder together about what is getting in the way of asking directly for what you need.

Changing your stance changes the dance. Standing in your vulnerability invites others to do the same (Brown 2015). Your journey toward wholeness invites others to embark on theirs. But it does not guarantee that they will. Be aware of your significant other's response to your vulnerable disclosures. Vulnerability deserves to be met honorably and without shaming, and vulnerable disclosures ought not to be used against you. The space between you holds the potential to be a crucible for witnessing, for truth, for accountability, and therefore for transformation. In my therapy office, I encourage clients to view vulnerable disclosures as sacred gifts that warrant the utmost respect in return.

Listening with the Third Ear

The power of these traps and reaches begins with you, but that's not where it ends. As Vietnamese Zen monk Thich Nhat Hanh offers, "When someone you love suffers, you're motivated to do something to help. But if you don't know how to handle the suffering in yourself, how can you help the other person to handle his suffering? We first have to handle the suffering in ourselves. Whenever a painful feeling or emotion arises, we should be able to be present with it—not fight it, but recognize it" (2011, 77).

So what happens when it's *your partner* who is using intimacy-preventing language? What can you do, especially when he or she is upset with you? When this happens, it is truly an invitation for your prefrontal cortex to show you what it's made of! Can this exquisite part of your brain keep you driving along the high road in the face of somebody else's upset? It is not easy to stay brave and open, especially because your partner's opinion of you is likely quite central to how you experience yourself. But it is possible.

When someone you care about is upset with you, you can ask yourself the question, "What would love do?" Love tries mightily to stay regulated even in the face of another's disappointment and upset. Love listens with *the third ear*—a term coined by psychoanalyst Theodor Reik. Listening with the third ear means listening in order to *understand* rather than listening in order to *respond*. Our default setting tends to be the latter: formulating our response while the other person talks. Yet what the other person seeks is not our response. It is our understanding—love manifest in the form of compassion. What an offering it is to suspend our ego's desire to explain, defend, and clarify in order to make space for the experience of another person!

When you listen with your third ear, you are truly a conduit of love. In addition, when you listen with your third ear in response to the other person's intimacy-preventing trap, you actually receive two gifts. First, you get the experience of witnessing firsthand how the fight-or-flight urge softens and transforms when met with steady love. Second, you get the experience of witnessing yourself behave in a brave and loving way. Everybody wins.

Love Languages

Another cushion-building practice is *respecting the power of love languages*. Relationship counselor and best-selling author Dr. Gary Chapman (2015) uses the term "love languages" to capture the idea that there is more than one way to give and receive love. Love speaks more than one language, and each of us has a preferred "tongue" for giving and receiving love. Love languages are *both* unique to the individual *and* impactful on the couple. I especially like how Dr. Chapman presents the five languages as simply different from each other. There is no hierarchy.

Here are the five languages of love, according to Dr. Chapman:

- Words of affirmation ("You are so talented.")

- Acts of service (doing the dishes even though it's not your turn)

- Giving/receiving gifts (surprising her with tickets to see Jay Z in concert)

- Quality time (dinner and a movie)

- Physical touch (hugging, back scratching, sex)

Disconnection happens when we, knowingly or unknowingly, value our own preferred love language above all others, judging our partners for not loving the way we do. Intimacy flows when we consciously give love in the language our partner can best receive it. And like everything else, our love language is often learned in the classroom of our childhood home.

I wish Todd and I had understood years ago how individual love languages impact intimate relationships, because it would have saved us a lot of drama. Here's an example. My mom's primary love language is giving and receiving gifts. As a kid, when my birthday approached, I would make a wish list. The day itself was a grand event, including meals of my choice—shrimp salad on cheesebread at Jacobson's for lunch, and spaghetti and meat sauce for dinner— and an elaborate "birthday table" of gifts.

Todd grew up in a family whose primary love language was quality time. Birthdays were a chance to gather together and do something fun, but gift giving was minimal and secondary. The differences in our primary love languages created plenty of misunderstandings in our early years. Imagine my disappointment when he gave me a balloon and a bag of gummy bears for my birthday. Imagine his confusion and discomfort when I would spend lots of time wrapping gifts for him. I wish we had known that love languages just *are*. Accepting and embracing the amazing *is-ness* (they are what they are) of love languages makes life so much easier.

Today, instead of buying gifts, I plan an adventure for Todd's birthday because I know, accept, and embrace that receiving gifts not only doesn't feel good but actually feels stressful to him. And we have agreed that if I would like a gift from him, I identify it, ask for it, and feel grateful if and when I receive it.

Respecting the power of love languages is as simple as it is profound. Identify your love language and humbly acknowledge that yours is not the best and only. Identify your partner's love language and be willing to "speak" it. Invite him or her to speak yours, but embrace that when love speaks to you in a language that is not your native one, it's still love. See how it feels when you welcome, rather than judge, love that speaks a little differently.

As Dr. Mona Fishbane's quote at the beginning of this lesson makes clear, intimate relationships invite us into a dynamic interdependence in which my choices and your choices commingle, like watercolors on canvas, changing us before our eyes. When I remain in touch with myself, I am responsible for my part of our dance, and the contributions I make can build the cushion of positivity and connection between us. I can expect and invite, but not demand, the same from you.

Steps Toward Loving Bravely

Build a cushion of relational positivity by committing to practices that embody love—choosing intimacy-inviting reaches and embracing unique love languages.

Traps and Reaches

The seven Intimacy-Preventing Traps identify which of these you are prone to using. Try practicing the intimacy-inviting reach that corresponds to your intimacy-preventing trap. When you are able to use an intimacy-inviting reach, give yourself lots of praise. These patterns are tough to change! How did the intimacy-inviting reach shift your emotions? How did your intimacy-inviting reach shift *the other person's* experience?

Love Language

What is your primary love language? You can take an online assessment in order to find out at: http://www.5lovelanguages.com. Is your love language the same as or different from the love languages spoken in your house when you were growing up? Reflect on your intimate relationships. Have differences in love languages been a source of tension? If so, how can you use this newly gained knowledge to handle these conflicts differently going forward?

Putting It All Together

The previous few lessons have explored some powerful ways of thinking about and navigating conflict, so this table is offered as a way of putting it all together. Review the table and circle what feels especially new and helpful to you.

Low Road	High Road
Linear conflict story	Systemic conflict story
Reactive	Vulnerable
Fight or flee	Embrace the pause
Self-protective survival strategies	Speak from vulnerability
Secondary feelings: angry, enraged, furious, insulted, agitated, irritable, disrespected	Primary feelings: sad, ashamed, lonely, inadequate, disappointed
Intimacy-preventing traps	Intimacy-inviting reaches

PART 4

Self-Expansion

Practice a Loving "I'm Sorry"

Beyond our ideas of right-doing and wrong-doing, there is a field.
I'll meet you there.

—Rumi

It has been seven weeks since Kevin's foot surgery. Although he's no longer in a cast, he still isn't able to walk or drive. His partner, Matt, has picked up a lot of slack around the house. And with two full-time jobs and two little kids, there is plenty of slack! One morning, after helping Kevin into the tub, Matt grabs his shaving cream.

"Ugh!" Matt groans. "What is this crust all over my shaving cream?"

Kevin fires back loudly, "If you have such a huge issue with me using your shaving cream, drive your butt to the store and buy another can!"

Matt puts his razor and shaving cream down on the counter and turns to face Kevin. "Excuse me?"

Kevin takes a deep breath, and his face softens. "I'm sorry, Matt. It's not you. It's this [pointing to his foot]. I am so sick of being immobilized. I feel awful about how hard you've been working. I'm just so done feeling like this!"

Matt comes over and kisses the top of his partner's head. "I know. I'm sick of it too. We will make it out alive. I promise!"

Kevin recounted this blowup at our therapy session, and I was aware that the apology he offered Matt was no small victory! Yes, he was the one who mishandled the shaving cream, and, yes, he was the one who blew up at Matt. It was pretty obvious that a heartfelt "I'm sorry" was his best move, but given Kevin's history, this was real progress.

Kevin grew up in a family that, as he says, "didn't do accountability." People neither gave nor took in feedback about the impact of their words and actions on other people. Feelings got stuffed deep down inside, and blowups like this one (if they happened at all) were just swept under the rug. Kevin's knee-jerk reaction to criticism—Matt's comment about the crust on the shaving cream—was to fight back, and that's what he did initially by telling Matt to go to the store. This is such an old and pervasive pattern, in fact, that Matt's nickname for Kevin is "Teflon" because nothing sticks to him. As Matt says, "Somehow, Kevin is never at fault."

What was different this time was that Kevin caught himself. He saw his knee-jerk reaction for what it was—a low-road response to feeling threatened. He course corrected and was able to quickly offer a heartfelt apology. Kevin has worked to grow his relational self-awareness. He can now see how his difficulty apologizing comes from his past and how it has a negative impact on his relationship with Matt. In fact, he really deeply *knows* how Matt feels when Kevin acts like Teflon because Kevin can recall how confusing and lonely it felt when he was on the receiving end of his parents' lack of accountability. Even though it was hard to learn a new way, Kevin wanted to break the cycle. He's proud when he is able to practice a new way.

Kevin's old story is: If you are critical of me, I don't trust that you can also still love me and hold me in high esteem. The urge to explain, defend, or argue back—the frantic effort to be valued—is still there inside of Kevin. But moments like this, when Kevin apologizes and Matt is able to offer him some comfort (a kiss on the head and assurance that they will get through this), are so healing for Kevin. It's neat to see how Kevin's willingness to apologize opened the door for him to receive what he most needed—to be reminded that he is loved, imperfections and all.

Kevin's apology was especially heartening given what he was going through. His physical pain and limitations have left him feeling on edge most of the time. He feels angry that he can't drive or exercise, guilty that his partner has to do so much, and ashamed that his partner has to help him bathe and get dressed. Under stress, all of us are more likely to fall back on less mature and less evolved ways of being in the world, so this chapter of his life is giving Kevin plenty of opportunities to work on being accountable for the impact of his behavior.

For his part, Matt's ability to accept Kevin's apology and move on instead of holding a grudge rested on his awareness that this is an area of great vulnerability for the man he loves. He has empathy for the dynamics that Kevin grew up with, he sees how much progress Kevin had made, and he trusts that Kevin will keep working on this core issue of his. Also, Matt is humble, knowing that he, too, is a work in progress. Even with this progress and deep commitment to their life together, Matt would never say this work is easy, but he would say it feels worthwhile.

The Field Beyond

We hurt those we love. For all kinds of reasons. Looking at how we hurt people we love is really hard work, kicking up incredibly uncomfortable feelings as we confront discrepancies between who we *believe* ourselves to be and who our actions suggest we are. The quote that opens this lesson, by 13th-century Sufi poet Rumi, offers a path that can help us tolerate this painful dialectic—I *both* love you *and* sometimes hurt you. Any confrontation of self about our hurtful behavior *must* take place in Rumi's field—the field out beyond right-doing and wrong-doing. The language of *bad* and *wrong* is simply a dead-end road, as those labels are really limiting. They cut off exploration, leading only to a call to action to "be different," which is too vague to be of service. Those labels also create shame, and shame is a lousy motivator of change.

In fact, simplistic labels like "good" and "bad" end up blocking us from being accountable for our behavior. My client, Val, is caught up in a good/bad story that actually *perpetuates* her hurtful behavior. She says that she does not want to look at her years-long pattern of cheating on her husband because she fears that she will discover that she is "a terrible person." I get that! I wouldn't want to look at my behavior either if my story was razor thin, containing only the possibility of "I am a terrible person" or "I am not a terrible person." She is held captive by her limited perspective, a perspective that prevents self-exploration because the stakes are so high. Exploring why she's engaging in behavior that at some level she knows is hurtful to her husband and their marriage means risking being stuck with a label that will create tons of shame. So her behavior persists. She opts for an *external* focus instead: she cheats because he's not affectionate, she cheats because there is no passion in the marriage, she cheats because she's lonely.

If we are going to look at our hurtful behavior, we *must* do it in Rumi's field. Self-confrontation has to take place there. When it does—when we are able to look at the choices we make that hurt the people we love—unforeseen possibilities for self-understanding and self-compassion emerge. And from that gentle field of space, change can happen. The dialectic here is: I am *both* worthy of gentleness *and* responsible for my impact on others. For Val, this would mean that she would begin to lovingly hold herself accountable for her behavior, moving from passive victim to empowered author of the life she wants. Therefore, rather than "bad" or "wrong," I find it helpful to talk about our hurtful behavior as *forgetful* or *unskilled*. This language allows us to be gentle with ourselves yet keeps us accountable for our actions.

"I Am Forgetful"

I believe that our true essence is love. I believe that for each and every one of us, our truest path is the Golden Rule: "Do unto others as you would have them do unto you." Therefore, when our behavior is not aligned with our true essence, we are behaving *forgetfully*. We are forgetting our true nature.

When we do something hurtful, and our behavior is framed this way, the questions are totally different. The questions are no longer "Am I a bad person?" and "Why am I a bad person?" The questions become *"What is keeping me from remembering who I truly am?"* and *"What is keeping me from treating my partner with love?"* These latter questions are infinitely more helpful. They invite change. The answers to these questions may lead to any number of change-producing actions: confronting your partner about ways you feel neglected or mistreated (causing you to do the same in return), asking for what you need in the relationship, taking better care of yourself, starting therapy, admitting to an addiction, and/or dealing with old trauma. From this softened place of expanded awareness, we can also more easily offer a heartfelt apology for our hurtful actions.

"I Am Unskilled"

Another shift that can make the "I'm sorry" flow more gently is viewing your behavior as *unskilled*. Kevin has benefited from this language. He hated looking at how much his difficulty with apologizing was hurting Matt. It stirred up a ton of defensiveness in him. And behind that defensiveness was a ton of shame—shame that led him to tell himself all kinds of stories about what an awful partner he is, how he doesn't deserve Matt, how he has messed up their life, and so on. The pendulum swung all the way from a blaming, no-apology stance to a shameful, I-am-worthless stance. And in both of these stances, Kevin pushed Matt away. In working on this issuue, Kevin found it helpful to frame his difficulty with apology as an unskilled behavior.

In therapy we talked about how he inherited a *triple threat* of sorts. First, he didn't see the adults in his house growing up taking responsibility for the impact of their actions. Second, in our Western culture, there is a notion that apologizing is a sign of weakness. Third, growing up male he internalized, in many direct and subtle ways, our society's prescribed masculine traits: "Keep the upper hand," "Keep a stiff upper lip," and "Never back down." These influences conspire to make apologizing difficult. When viewed as a *skill* he needs to learn in order to improve his relationship, practicing apologizing becomes *prideful* instead of shameful for him.

Heartfelt Apologies 101

My husband, Todd, finds the topic of this lesson terribly amusing, as offering a heartfelt apology is, shall we say, challenging for me. Like all of us, I remain ever a work in progress. I have learned that when you roll your eyes and put your hand on your hip as you say, "I'm sorry," you negate the apology entirely! I also have learned that the degree to which I am able to greet my imperfections with gentleness is the degree to which I am able to apologize with full eye contact, steady hips, and an open heart. Here are some ideas to keep in mind:

- You can offer a heartfelt apology if the *impact* is that you hurt someone even if you did not *intend* to hurt them. Intent and impact have little to do with each other.

- You can apologize for something even if you think the other person should not feel hurt and even if you would not feel hurt if the roles were reversed.

- Your apology does not mean that the other person is simply an innocent victim. We often hurt others because we feel they hurt us first, but it turns out this fact does not really matter all that much. Your apology means that you are taking responsibility for *your* part. At a different time, you may ask your partner to acknowledge and apologize for how *his or her* actions hurt you.

- When you apologize, you are acknowledging to yourself, to the other person, and to the entire universe that you know you are not perfect. The more deeply you embrace your imperfections, the happier and healthier you will be. So apologizing helps your partner, it helps the relationship, *and* it helps you. A heartfelt "I'm sorry" packs quite a punch!

- If you say, "I'm sorry, but…" (and then offer an explanation, an excuse, or a counter-complaint about the other person), the "but" negates the whole apology. The "but" is the verbal equivalent of the hand on the hip or the eye roll. "I'm sorry" is a complete sentence.

- Try to focus your apology on *doing* rather than *being*. In other words, apologize for your actions ("I yelled" or "I forgot") instead of apologizing for who you are as a person ("I am rageful" or "I am neglectful").

- Sometimes we say, "I'm sorry," when we should be saying, "Thank you." For example, you call your partner in a panic because you received a negative review from your supervisor. At the end of the call, instead of saying, "I'm sorry I took up so much of your time," try saying, "Thank you for being here for me."

Amends Action

Some heartfelt apologies need to be paired with an *amends action*. An amends action is something you do in order to demonstrate your understanding of the impact of your hurtful behavior. In fact, research indicates that the acknowledgment of responsibility and offering to repair are the most important ingredients in an apology (Lewicki, Polin, and Lount 2016). Amends actions move you from talking the talk to walking the walk. I remember hearing an example of a man who gave up alcohol for a year as an amends action for cheating on his partner. This was his attempt to *embody* his apology, and, as the story goes, his amends action really helped his partner.

She felt he was taking their healing journey seriously, which energized her to do her part—the difficult work of forgiving.

Another form of amends action happens when a couple works together to figure out what needs to change between them. For example, when there has been dishonesty about money, a couple may decide to grant each other access to bank account information. Or when there has been infidelity, a couple may create new and different boundaries like sharing passwords or checking in more frequently when they are apart. Amends actions foster trust when they are initiated by the one who is apologizing. Amends actions can breed resentment when the one who is apologizing waits passively to have "rules" given to him or her. The online "Guide to Heartfelt Apologies and Forgiveness" (http://www.newharbinger.com/35814) provides a review of this material.

I'm Sorry—Good-bye

Sometimes I work with couples who seek therapy in the eleventh hour, so to speak, and sometimes the decision to end the relationship is made right there in my office. Depending on how adversarial the breakup is, the therapy may continue for a while, and we may do some wrap-up or termination work. Couples have found it meaningful to create ending rituals that can be devoted to mutual apologies: "I see how I hurt you. Here are the ways that I was not able to be the person you needed me to be."

This is a high-wire act for sure, and most of us can only touch that expansive place for small windows of time before the complexity of our emotional world swallows us up again. But even after that moment has passed, you forever have the memory of witnessing yourself standing in humble accountability. I think this is what people mean when they say they want "closure." They want the opportunity to hear the other person validate their story of the relationship. Your chances of receiving that closure are greatly increased if you are willing to give validation of the other person's story as well.

The Limits of an Apology

In closing, even a heartfelt apology can do only so much. Know that your healing is not contingent upon whether the other person is ready to hear or accept your apology. If you are able to offer an apology in humility and truth, then you have reached the outer edge of what you can control. Attempting to "get them to listen," even though it is driven by your pain and your shame, is a *boundary violation*, reflecting that you have exited your own business and entered the business of another.

Your business is to offer the apology. The other person's business is to decide what to do with it. Stay present with *your* emotional journey and *your* ever-expanding awareness, trusting these to grow your ability to be more relationally skilled and better able to embody your truest essence going forward.

Steps Toward Loving Bravely

The degree to which you can offer a heartfelt "I'm sorry" to another is the degree to which you can humbly embrace your imperfect nature, neither melting into shame nor hardening into blame.

Apology Template

How we relate to the act of apologizing is shaped by what we learned growing up. Take a look at the section "Heartfelt Apologies 101" (or download and print the handout at http://www.newharbinger .com/35814) and put a star next to the ideas that were and are part of your family of origin's apology story. Reflect on how you have internalized these aspects of apology and how they help you in your relationships today. Notice the ideas that you *did not* put a star next to—the things you didn't learn from your family about apologizing. Which of these remain difficult for you in your relationships today? What are your apology growing edges (what can you get better at)?

Apology Story

Write about a time when you had to apologize to someone you cared about for something that you had said or done. Answer these questions:

- What happened? (Tell the story of what led up to your hurtful behavior, tell the story of your hurtful behavior, and tell the story of the aftermath.)

- How did you know that you needed to apologize?

- In what ways was it difficult for you to apologize? In what ways was it easy or seamless for you to apologize?

- To what extent did you find yourself attempting to change the other person's opinion or perception of you? Toward what end? What was painful to you about the other person's opinion or perception of you?

- In what ways did you (either with the other person or on your own) explore the difference between intent and impact? What was helpful about that?

- Was there an amends action? What did you commit to within yourself going forward? What did that experience teach you about how you want to be in the world?

Working with Apology Growing Edges

Ask someone you trust to talk with you about what it's like for him or her to give you feedback about your behavior. In other words, when you do something that hurts this person's feelings, what is it like for him or her to approach you with it? How open or defensive does he or she find you to be?

Forgive…Again and Again

Forgiveness is another name for freedom.

—Byron Katie

Years ago, I decided to include a unit on forgiveness in our "Marriage 101" course, and as I dove more deeply into the topic, it became clear to me that forgiveness is germane to all human relationships, and certainly all intimate relationships. Just as we must know how to offer a heartfelt apology when we hurt someone we care about, in order to fall in love and to stay in love, we must understand how to forgive someone when he or she has hurt us. Yes, forgiveness finds its way into all of our intimate relationships. This lesson about forgiveness follows from the previous lesson about apology. Apology and forgiveness exist in a sacred relationship with each other. The former opens the door for the latter, even though we know that sometimes apologies are not accepted, and sometimes forgiveness occurs in the absence of an apology.

What Forgiveness Is and Isn't

Forgiveness is a canceled debt (Markman and Stanley 2010). This definition acknowledges that you *could* keep the person who hurt you in debt to you. You are entitled to do that. But instead you are choosing to cancel the debt. I like how this definition reminds us that forgiveness is active. Forgiveness means that you have made a choice. Oprah Winfrey says that "forgiveness means letting go of the wish that the past could be different." When we have been hurt, our instinct is to wish, deeply and fully, that the violation had not happened. But that wish creates suffering because, indeed, it did happen and it cannot un-happen. We are left only with the present moment and the future. In this way, forgiveness is truly the centerpiece of all healing.

Forgiveness is a gift that you give yourself. When you forgive someone who has hurt you, it says *nothing* about the offense itself. It does *not* mean that you think the offense was no big deal. It does *not* excuse the other person's behavior. A lack of forgiveness is quite lousy for your emotional and physical health (see, for example, Lawler-Row et al. 2008), so forgiveness frees *you* from the chains of resentment and simmering anger. We know that some people find it essential to forgive horrendous violations like assault, abuse, and murder of a loved one, not because the offender "deserves" their forgiveness, but in order to save their own lives and sanity.

So, how does forgiveness happen? Think back to that bucket of navy blue paint from lesson 14. We can use that metaphor again here, imagining this time that the bucket of navy blue paint is my story of the hurt: what happened; my emotional pain; and what I believe it says about me, about the other person, and about the world. Forgiveness is the white paint—when mixed in, it transforms the very story itself. As I forgive, my story transforms. Over time and with my commitment to forgive, when I think about that chapter of my life, I may still feel emotional pain, but I will not experience *suffering*, which is arguing with reality and remaining stuck in a thin story about how it "should not" have happened. As the story changes, who I am in the story transforms as well. Rather than the passive stance of a *victim*, I move toward the active and empowered stance of a *survivor*.

At the risk of offering one metaphor too many, here's another for you to think about. When we make the choice to forgive someone, it is more as if we are *in recovery* than *cured*. A while ago, I had a serious neck injury. I did all the things I needed to get better: apply ice, get rest, and do physical therapy. It took many months, and today I am back to doing all the activities and exercises that I was doing before I was injured. But I would not say that I'm cured. I would say that I am in recovery. If I push myself too hard at the gym or if I sleep in a funky position, I feel pain. I also need to be a little more careful with that part of my body. Forgiveness is like this. The pain lessens over time, but we may remain especially vulnerable to "stuff" that touches us in that same place.

My client, Charles, is recovering but is not cured. He has forgiven his father for abandoning him and his mother when he was ten years old, yet like an old injury, emotional pain still gets stirred up from time to time. For example, when his own son turned ten, Charles experienced bouts of rage and sadness—"How could he leave me when I was ten? I feel how much my son needs me in his life!" It is helpful for Charles to be gentle with himself when he experiences these waves of emotion, as he knows that telling himself to "get over it already" will not work. He acknowledges that he is in recovery and that, although he has forgiven his father, emotional pain remains. He tries to stay present with the emotions as they arise, trusting their ebb and flow, and he works on *parenting himself from the inside*—offering empathy to his ten-year-old self. In doing so, he is able to focus attention on what his presence offers to his own son, and he swells with gratitude and pride for his relational heroism (Real 1998).

Forgiveness is not like flipping a switch. Even if our minds demand, "Forgive!" our hearts may have a different timeline. Forgiving cannot happen all at once because, well, hurt hurts! In fact, research has found that there is overlap between the parts of our brains that code physical pain and the parts that code emotional pain (Johnson 2013). All pain is real and must be honored. Yet it is also the case that we cannot simply sit around passively and wait for forgiveness to simply arrive. The process that Charles uses—naming and connecting with negative emotions when they arise—is helpful. Focusing on what you feel grateful for also helps. Meditation is a powerful tool that can help you move from a place of resentment and pain toward a place of forgiveness. Research indicates that mindfulness, which is cultivated through meditation, can aid forgiveness (Johns, Allen, and Gordon 2015). You'll find a forgiveness meditation at the end of this lesson.

Forgiving an Ex: Punished for a Crime She Didn't Commit

Forgiveness after an intimate relationship has ended is important work, as there is an internal and a relational price paid when we *withhold* forgiveness. If you have not forgiven your ex for hurting you, you risk bringing that old pain into your next intimate relationship, unfairly punishing your new partner for a crime that he or she did not commit. Forgiving your ex—regardless of whether he or she did anything to warrant it—frees *you* up from the chains of the past so that you can love again.

Holding on to the pain of the past can be an effort to stay safe and protected going forward, but the consequence is that your new partner is fighting a ghost. We have no choice but to enter an intimate relationship fully, trusting our resilience if we should happen to fall. Loving bravely involves sharing with your new partner the ways in which your old pain has left you "in recovery," so that you can advocate for what you need, such as transparency and truthful communication. This courageous path is quite different from the hypervigilant and defensive stance that inevitably results when old fears and lack of forgiveness are in the driver's seat.

Forgiveness, Boundaries, Resentment, and Acceptance

People use the aphorism "forgive and forget," but I don't think the "forget" part is possible, necessary, or advisable. When you choose to maintain a relationship with the person who has hurt you, you both will need to be mindful and careful going forward. For example, when I am doing therapy with a couple recovering from infidelity, forgetting would not be a very smart thing to do! Both partners need to talk about what kinds of safeguards make sense—for example, sharing passwords, reducing alcohol consumption, or staying with friends instead of in a hotel when traveling alone for business. Protecting the relationship from the risk of further hurt is an essential aspect of forgiveness.

Forgiveness and boundaries dance together, playing off of each other. If I have been hurt by your behavior, I ought to reflect on what kind of boundary I need in our relationship going forward. If I forgive you and then we manage that boundary effectively, what is yielded is *acceptance*. I can accept you as you are (and the situation as it is) because I am managing my boundaries in a way that allows me to connect with you while protecting myself. If I forgive you but *do not* effectively manage the boundary between us going forward, I am likely to end up feeling violated again, which will breed feelings of *resentment* within me.

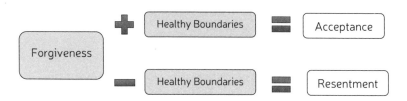

Let's look at this dance in action. A friend of mine was talking about how he and his wife have learned to manage her chronic tardiness. When they have plans to go out for the evening, he gets ready in a timely fashion. She does not. For a long time, he would feel stressed out and hurt. He took her behavior personally, feeling that if she loved him, she would be ready on time. He would behave impatiently—reminding her of the time, asking her to hurry, and stomping around the house. She would fight back—assuring him that she'd be ready soon, telling him to relax, and labeling him as controlling. Sometimes their whole evening would be ruined over this time-management problem. He found himself feeling quite resentful.

He tried to forgive her for not being ready on time, telling himself, "She is imperfect, just like me." He tried to not take her behavior personally. He tried to be more patient. However, none of that helped. He still ended up feeling resentful. So he came up with a new plan. Now once he is ready, he makes himself a drink and a really nice appetizer, and then he reads a book or watches TV. Along with forgiving her for being imperfect, he also needed to add a *healthy boundary*. He takes care of himself by starting the evening off without her—but with some wine and cheese. He has found that by adding the boundary, instead of resentment, he feels a sense of *acceptance*. In an interesting footnote, his decision to add a boundary in this way has led to a change in his wife's behavior. She doesn't want him to start the festivities without her, so she gets ready faster. Love is nothing if not a dance!

We face questions about forgiveness on matters ranging from *the ordinary* (How do I cope with a chronically tardy partner?) to *the profound* (Do I need to forgive my father for sexually abusing me in order to heal? Should I forgive my fiancé for hitting me?). When it comes to profound forgiveness questions like these, know that the path to clarity is tender and deeply personal. Questions like these are best answered in collaboration with a mental health professional who specializes in working with trauma. Appendix 1 has more information about trauma, and appendix 2 has information about finding a therapist.

Although each person's journey to healing from abuse is unique, there are some common elements. Survivors need to work on managing their relational boundaries in order to ensure their own physical and emotional safety. Survivors need to grieve the loss of who they were (and what they believed about the world) before the abuse occurred. Finally, if a survivor's suffering involves self-blame for any aspect of the abuse (for not telling anybody, for staying in the relationship, and so on), he or she will need self-forgiveness. This forgiveness work is separate and apart from whether and how he or she forgives the abuser.

Trusting Your Resilience

We know that forgiveness is a process, not a one-time event. We know that "forgive and forget" is neither possible nor desirable. And we know that, for our own good, we ought to forgive someone who has hurt us even when we are no longer in a relationship with him or her. Even though withholding forgiveness can make us feel safe, as if we are behind a shield of sorts, our least desirable course of action is to remain in a relationship while stuck in simmering resentment.

Forgiving someone and remaining in a relationship with that person is brave, as it requires vulnerability. It requires us to ask for what we need, and it requires us to take the emotional risk of getting back into the ring (Brown 2015). And the truth is, even when we do everything we can to ensure healing—including accountability, boundaries, and amends actions—we may still be hurt again, reminding us that the ultimate trusting relationship must be with ourselves. We must be willing to say, "I trust my wisdom in staying and forgiving, and I trust my resilience to get up if I am knocked down again."

Steps Toward Loving Bravely

Understanding when and how to forgive frees you from the past, allowing you to show up fully for the present.

Family Grudges

Write a journal entry about what you saw when you were growing up regarding forgiveness. Write down three things you were you taught *explicitly* or directly about forgiveness from family, friends, school, and/or religious education. Then write down three things you learned about forgiveness just by watching the adults in your life. Did the people who raised you hold grudges—remaining stuck in a lack of forgiveness? Or, at the other extreme, did they get stuck in cycles of mistreatment because they struggled to hold others accountable for their actions?

What Gets in the Way?

Write about a time when you needed to forgive someone. First, tell the story of what happened—how were you hurt? Next, write about the accountability process (if there was one). Did you bring the issue to the other person's attention? Did the other person bring the issue to your attention? Did you ask for an apology, or did the other person volunteer an apology?

Perhaps there was *no* accountability process, and you needed to find a way to forgive that person anyway. If this was the case, write about what you think got in the way of the other person being accountable for his or her actions and apologizing to you. What blocked his or her apology? For example, was the other person blocked by a cultural, gendered, or family story that says apologizing would make him or her "lose face" or appear "weak"? Was the other person blocked by a story that he or she did nothing wrong and you were "overreacting"—in other words, not able to distinguish between intent and impact?

Finally, write about your process of forgiving that person. What helped you forgive that person? What got in the way? How do you feel today when this painful issue comes to mind? How is your feeling today different from how you felt about the issue before you were able to forgive?

Perhaps writing about this is bringing to your awareness that you are struggling to forgive the other person. If this is the case, what can you use from this lesson to help you move toward forgiveness for your own sake and for the sake of your intimate relationship—now or going forward?

Building Your Forgiveness Muscles

One of the most gifted and beloved teachers of meditation, Jack Kornfield (2016), offers the following forgiveness meditation. Find a comfortable and quiet place to sit. Quiet your mind, breathe into the area around your heart, and begin to recite these words. As you recite them, stay present with the images and feelings that come up. Recite this meditation until you feel a shift within yourself: a release, an opening, a softening.

There are many ways that I have been harmed by others, abused or abandoned, knowingly or unknowingly, in thought, word, or deed. I now remember the many ways others have hurt or harmed me, wounded me, out of fear, pain, confusion, and anger. I have carried this pain in my heart too long. To the extent that I am ready, I offer them forgiveness. To those who have caused me harm, I offer my forgiveness, I forgive you.

Practice this meditation regularly until you notice that when you think of the person and the situation, you feel less emotionally upset (angry, sad, or afraid) and more neutral or peaceful. You can find this meditation, along with other reminders about apologizing and forgiving, in the online "Guide to Heartfelt Apologies and Forgiveness" at http://www.newharbinger.com/35814. Know that even if you move yourself into a more forgiving place right now, events down the road may stir up old pain. This practice will be here for you if and when that happens!

Lesson 18

Value Presence

Each time you love, love as deeply as if it were forever.

—Audre Lorde

As my best friend, Alexandra Folz (whose poetic words open this book), says, "Presence is hard work." I agree. I think about *presence* as the degree to which we are *in* an interaction with another person. The degree to which we are "showing up." Like in the old-school game, the Hokey Pokey, think about whether just part of you is present ("I put my right foot in") or all of you is present ("I put my whole self in"). When we are working to be fully present with someone, we are paying attention with our *minds* so that we can listen and contribute, and we are paying attention with our *hearts* so that we can empathize. The energy of presence is powerful. It grows love. Offering our heartfelt presence to another person creates love and nurtures love. We know this in our bones.

Despite the fact that we intuitively know this, presence seems to be in short supply these days. We are living in an incredibly fast-paced digital age, which has created a strange irony. Between online dating, texting, and social media, we are arguably more *connected* than ever before (Turkle 2015). But we also seem to be less *present* than ever before. Listening while texting. Texting while watching a show. Watching a show while scrolling Facebook. We seem to rarely put our whole self in one place at one time. Technology has become an integral part of every aspect of our lives—even our love lives. It is not uncommon for therapy clients to bring out their phones midsession in order to read me a text exchange they had with their intimate partner. We look for love online, and we conduct the business of love online as well!

This lesson will expand your awareness about how our collective love affair with our handheld devices affects our ability to be present for love. Presence *is* indeed hard work, but it is work worth doing in order to love and be loved. (Just a heads-up: I promise not to trash technology or urge you to throw out your phone. I'm quite enamored with mine!)

Technology and Love: A Square Peg in a Round Hole

I have begun to offer workshops about technology and love, which is a fun topic to talk about because it's so relevant, complex, and confusing. I feel clear that some of our current difficulties in love stem from the fact that we have become quite entwined with our devices. Therefore, we seem to be importing our experiences with and our expectations of technology into our love lives. It's as if our storylines have become confused, resulting in a square-peg-round-hole situation. These two things that just don't fit together. We have to make sure we understand the differences between the *energy of technology* and the *energy of love*. The following table helps us discern one type of "energy" from the other.

The Energy of Technology	The Energy of Love
All about *me*	All about *we*
Consumers	Givers or servers
More (more distraction, more choice)	Less (less distraction, less choice)

New and better	Commitment, acceptance, and gratitude
Fast and efficient	Requires time to grow and time to maintain
Doing	Being
Answers	Mysteries and paradoxes

Let's look at each of these contrasts:

- **Technology is self-centered.** It's all about *me* and it's all about consuming. Yes, I know that people all over the world use technology in order to serve humanity and care for our planet, but many of our day-to-day interactions with our devices are about our individual needs and wants. *Love is us-centered.* In an intimate relationship, we must shift to a "we" perspective, caring for the space between partners and figuring out how to optimize individual happiness while tending to the relationship.

- **Technology promises newer, better, faster.** The moment I see your new phone, mine suddenly seems clunky and retro by comparison, and I want to upgrade ASAP, craving the rush of novelty. *Love offers acceptance, gratitude, and commitment.* Intimate relationships require us to commit and then invest and nurture what we already have for the long term.

- **Technology purports efficiency and convenience.** High-speed Internet, time-saving apps, and goods delivered right to our doorstep. People even say they opt for online dating in order to save time and hassle. In my more cynical moments, I feel quite discouraged about our quest to streamline our intimate relationships—what could we possibly be doing that is more valuable than giving and receiving love? My students insist that technology helps them weed out the people they wouldn't want to connect with so that they can get to the giving and receiving love part more quickly! I suppose we must agree to disagree. **Love springs from growth and maintenance work.** Love is not about efficiency. Love requires time to grow—you couldn't possibly feel about someone on the fourth date the way you will feel about him or her on your five-year anniversary.

- **Technology is about doing.** It is goal-driven, task-oriented, and purposeful, getting us from A to B. **Love is about being.** While couples certainly do all kinds of things together, the heart of an intimate relationship is about being—being present, being together, being witnesses to each other's lives.

- **Technology gives us answers.** We use technology to seek answers to so many of life's questions, both big and small, from seeking medical advice and driving directions to remembering the name of that actress in that film we adored. **Love requires us to welcome mystery and paradox.** In our intimate relationships, very little is ever solved, fixed, or answered. Instead, loving and being loved teaches us how to sit ever more comfortably with an unknown, with agreeing to disagree, and with places of multiple truths.

So what are we to do? How do we make use of all of what technology has to offer without short-changing what is needed to support the flourishing of love? The answer is not to throw out our phones or wax poetic about the good ol' days. The answer, I believe, is to practice *discernment*—to make choices from a place of conscious awareness. When we catch ourselves expecting from love what we expect from technology—efficiency, ease, speed—we can *name* that ("There I go again, expecting something unrealistic from my intimate relationship"), and we can remind ourselves that we have no choice but to embrace (or at least tolerate) the messiness of love.

We can also start expecting more from ourselves and each other and do the vast majority of our loving face-to-face, not screen-to-screen. How about using technology simply as a means of getting from here to there and nothing more, viewing online communication simply as a vehicle for getting us to the same space at the same time ("Let's meet for lunch at noon")?

I find it troubling that couples are increasingly opting to have their fights online, a phenomenon that Dr. Sheri Turkle writes about in her book *Reclaiming Conversation* (2015). People prefer fighting by text for a couple reasons. There will be a transcript they can look back on of who said what to whom, and conflict feels less messy and out of control because they can think about what they want to say before sending. Yet, what is the price we pay for these perceived benefits? What is lost? These longings—for an accountability record and for neatness—reflect that we have muddied our story of technology and our story of love. As we know, conflict is to be *navigated*, not *eliminated*. Intimacy, indeed our very humanity, is found in those rich and messy places—a foot that meets another foot as a peace offering, a compassionate gaze that softens an angry heart. *Our bodies and our faces speak a language that no emoji can ever hope to capture.* Our bravest work in love is to remember and to honor the power of our presence.

"Little p" Presence

Honoring the power of presence requires us to grow our self-awareness about two separate but related ideas. I call these ideas *"little p" presence* and *"big P" Presence*.

- "Little p" presence is about how we show up for little moments, for microinteractions.

- "Big P" Presence is about how we show up for an intimate relationship, how much we are in the Hokey Pokey of love.

Our "little p" presence is very important in our intimate relationships, but it is subtle and a bit sneaky. Researchers have found that when two people have a conversation in the presence of a cell phone, feelings of interpersonal closeness and trust are significantly compromised. They report feeling less empathy and understanding from each other (Przybylski and Weinstein 2012). It seems that we pay a pretty steep price for our desire to be connected at all times. Afraid to miss something *out there*, we end up missing something *right here*, trading our "little p" presence for some vague and ephemeral connection in "phone world" (Ansari 2015).

When it comes to our technology, it turns out that we tend to have a double standard, desiring the full attention of another while giving only a portion of our own. I'm guilty of this. I sometimes feel neglected and disrespected if Todd checks his e-mail as I'm talking to him, but if he asks me to put down my phone as he talks, I tend to get a bit defensive, sure that I can adequately attend to him while also scrolling my Instagram feed. But I can't. None of us can. Multitasking does not work, and our intimate relationships need and deserve our "little p" presence. As Turkle (2015) says, "Think of unitasking as the next big thing" (321). See the online guide "Technology Best Practices" for support in bringing your whole self to your relationships (http://www.newharbinger.com/35814).

"Big P" Presence

"Big P" presence is about commitment. For those who are looking for love, the wonders of technology offer a quantity of potential partners that was unimaginable a generation or two ago. No longer limited to the guy or gal next door, today we can cast a wide net in our search for love. Although this fact is not problematic in and of itself, there are consequences to loving in the age of abundance, and, as usual, relational self-awareness is our best compass.

It turns out that more is not necessarily better. In his 2004 book *The Paradox of Choice*, psychologist Barry Schwartz cites research showing that our desire for variety ends up reducing our feelings of satisfaction once we have made a choice. More options tend not to make us feel happier. Comedian and astute observer of culture, Aziz Ansari, applied Schwartz's ideas to the world of intimate relationships in his book *Modern Romance* (2015). Seduced into thinking that more choice is better, we spend countless hours on dating apps, shopping for love in a manner not completely unlike the manner in which we shop for shoes and wondering whether Mr. or Ms. Right is just one more swipe away. We must remember that at the other end of that profile is a living, breathing, three-dimensional human being, just like us.

Once in an intimate relationship, instead of asking, "Am I happy here?" we seem to be increasingly asking the question, "Could I be happier somewhere else?" (Perel 2015). This consumer mentality (Doherty 2013) doesn't serve our intimate relationships very well. When we decide to make a commitment to one person and go through relational rituals (moving in together, becoming engaged and so on), it is essential to trust ourselves to have made a *good-enough choice* of a partner and cultivate happiness *within* that relationship. Instead of looking for all the places where "the grass may be greener," commitment to another person means that we choose to weed and water our own yard (Markman and Stanley 2010). This is not about settling. It is about making the conscious choice to focus on what you like, love, and admire about your partner and to defocus on the rest.

Yes, we live in an era of choice, from an entire aisle full of breakfast cereal (unheard of a generation ago) to dating apps that offer a seemingly endless lineup of potential mates. *But love is about pairing up by paring down.* Love is about committing to "the one," honoring the fact that even though we know we could keep looking, we choose "us." One of my students shared with me that she and her girlfriend ritualized an important step in their commitment to each other by lighting a candle, opening a bottle of wine, and deleting all of their online dating apps. Lovely! "Big P" Presence is about being able to say, "I know there are other people out there, and other relationships that I could create, but I choose this one."

In order to love fully and bravely, we must be willing to offer our "big P" Presence to the one we are with, symbolically and concretely letting go of the "what ifs." This takes guts, doesn't it? It is tempting to keep a little thread of a storyline open with a couple of other people just in case it doesn't work out, but this is not our bravest path. Unless we want our partner to keep outside dialogue with other potential mates while committing to us, we are better off practicing the Golden Rule. In addition, it is a self-fulfilling prophecy. If we do not put our "whole self" in, we do not truly give love its best chance of success. Even if we wish it were otherwise, intimate relationships are fragile and need the protection of "big P" Presence to take root and grow.

There is another aspect of "big P" Presence that is more subtle than relationship commitment—an aspect that is about being present to the possibility in front of you. You don't have to be in a committed relationship to be present! Woven into the very definition of dating is the process of weighing options, imagining possibilities, and making comparisons. Dating means spending time communicating online with people and going on (maybe lots of) first dates. Dating is about exploring, and as you explore, let self-awareness be your greatest guide. *Self-aware dating* means valuing presence—both little and big. It's easy to see how "little p" presence is useful on a date. By keeping your phone silenced and put away, you can bring your full attention to the interaction between you and your date, which will help you access the vital data from within your gut—your deep and wise intuitive knowing.

But does it seem strange that "big P" Presence—putting our whole self in—would also apply to dating? A graduate student of mine shared with me a piece of advice that had been given to her by a dating coach: *follow one storyline through to the end.* This piece of advice is an invitation to "big P" Presence. Rather than going on three first dates a week, which, thanks in part to technology, is entirely possible, pursue one possibility at a time. This requires restraint and willingness to stand outside of our cultural belief that more is better. Following one storyline through allows the possibility of bringing your fullest self to this exact moment, this very opportunity. Rather than checking your matches in the bathroom on your first date, what happens when you suspend everything else that is happening and bring your full self to this possibility?

If part of you is protesting this idea—"But she is also probably checking her matches in the bathroom! It's just what's done!"—take a moment and sink into how this would feel in reverse. When I imagine someone checking matches while on a date with me, I feel hurt and ashamed, as if I am somehow not enough, even for just an evening. Even still, it is not easy to offer something to someone when we are not sure it is what we are getting in return—sort of like a game of Vulnerability Hot Potato. Who will offer their presence first? At moments like this, when I want to hold myself to a certain standard yet I am not sure the other person will, I find it helpful to think about the Mahatma Gandhi quote, "Be the change you wish to see in the world." I can embody what I desire in return. So, here, "big P" Presence doesn't necessarily mean "till death do us part." Here, "big P" Presence is about stepping into the possibility of love by being fully with the one who is in front of us, right here, right now.

Steps Toward Loving Bravely

Love is created and nurtured when we bring our attention to the present moment, and in the digital age, this is more precious and difficult than ever.

My Phone and Me

Take this opportunity to do a fearless moral inventory (Alcoholics Anonymous lingo) about your relationship with your phone by creating a table with three columns: Before/During/After. Over the next few days, take notes on this table about how you feel before, during, and after you scroll through social media. Make sure in your notes that you include any specific observations you have about the impact that your use of social media has on your intimate relationship. As you look over the data you have collected, what do you notice? What feels troubling? What feels reassuring?

Technology Best Practices

Based on what you learned in the previous exercise about your relationship with your phone, identify which of the following practices would help you live with more presence. Select two or three from the list below and stick with them!

- **Unitasking:** If you are talking to someone, talk to someone. If you are watching a show, watch a show. If you are checking Facebook, check Facebook. Take one task to completion before beginning the next one.

- **The boring bits:** Related to the unitasking challenge, see what happens if you opt not to use your phone to mindlessly fill in the "boring bits" (Turkle 2015). For example, when you are in the checkout line at the grocery store, instead of looking at your phone, look around, daydream, ponder, or strike up a conversation with the cashier or the customer next to you. Feeling competent and confident at small talk is important for those looking for love as well as for those in love.

- **Increasing intervals:** Set an interval for how often you can check your phone that is *longer* than the interval you have now. For example, if you check every ten minutes, challenge yourself to check every twenty minutes.

- **Phone home:** Leave your phone in one central place in your home instead of carrying it around with you.

- **Shut it down:** Choose a daily technology end time, maybe an hour before you go to sleep.

- **Stimulus control:** Especially if you are online dating, put the business of checking your matches on stimulus control. Instead of mindlessly checking on the train to work and in your dentist's waiting room, create a ritual for checking. Love is sacred and deserves nothing less. Check at a particular time, in a particular place—for example, after dinner on your balcony.

Putting Your Whole Self In

Write about the degree to which you embody "big P" (presence) in your life. When on a date, how fully do you show up? To what degree do you find your attention wandering? To what degree do you find yourself feeling closed off and defensive? To what degree do you allow yourself to imagine the possibility of building a relationship with this person? To what degree do you compare this person to another, a process that takes you out of the moment?

When you are in an intimate relationship with someone, to what degree are you able to commit yourself to the relationship? To what degree do you keep other possibilities open (via online or other kinds of communication)? What is the story that supports that behavior? What are the thoughts and feelings that come up for you around commitment? What makes it difficult for you to put your whole self in—fear of getting hurt, thoughts that someone better might come along, and so forth? What is the impact of not fully entering the intimate relationship—on you, on the other person, and on the relationship itself?

Lesson 19

Be on Your Own Team

One of the best guides to how to be self-loving is to give ourselves the love we are often dreaming about receiving from others.

—bell hooks

We are stuck. Again. I sit in session and watch Nicole turn away from Andrew, her shoulders slumped and her head heavy with defeat. "There's just nothing I can say or do. Nothing." Andrew and I hold eye contact for a long time, and I say, "Andrew, I can only imagine how alone you must feel right now. Nicole wants nothing more than to be with you as you two face this problem. To partner with you. She's knocking on your door, but it's so hard for you to let her in, isn't it?"

It is clear to me that the weight of Andrew's shame is crushing him, and I am afraid that it is slowly killing their relationship. He has been unemployed for many months; her part-time job and his parents' contributions keep them afloat. He is irritable most of the time, and she feels as if she is walking on eggshells. She is frustrated and lonely. Her true essence is problem-solver and cheerleader, and I am impressed by the fact that she does not blame him or shame him. From her perspective, this is *their* problem—their choices got them into this mess, and both of them need to get themselves out of it.

Andrew does not share this perspective. He is drowning in shame, yet he struggles mightily when I use that word—instead he prefers to talk about feeling stressed and feeling mad at himself. From his perspective, he has screwed up big-time, and his joblessness reflects his inadequacy. Therefore, anything Nicole says or does—forwarding a job posting to him, offering to edit his résumé, inquiring about the family budget—feels to him like an assault. It is as if Andrew is stuck in a deep and dark hole, and Nicole is on the ground above, desperate to be with her partner, as she knows he's suffering tremendously. Her questions, comments, and concerns are *intended* to be tools—a flashlight, a rope, a ladder that can help him out, or at least a snack to keep his energy up. Tragically, her attempts to be involved feel to Andrew as if she is throwing rocks into the hole or taunting him. So he responds critically and defensively, sighing and saying something like, "You don't get it. That's never going to work!" Nicole goes back to biting her tongue and continuing to tiptoe, giving Andrew what he says he needs—space to figure it out on his own.

When Nicole retreats, she is left without a partner and terrified about the future. And when she leaves Andrew in the hole, their relationship grows ever more distant. And guess what else happens? Andrew's shame wins. Again. She walks away, and he spends another long day trapped with his shame telling him this is *exactly* where he belongs. Andrew is embroiled in the fight of his life, and the very tool he needs is one for which he has tremendous contempt. That tool? *Self-compassion.*

Self-compassion is the only way out of that hole. Self-compassion is the only way he will be able to let Nicole near him. Without it, he will keep her at arm's length because it's too risky. Even if she could be a gentle, totally empathic, perfectly attuned angel every moment of every day, Andrew's shame would continue to stand guard, looking for the slightest evidence that she is belittling and undermining him. In the absence of self-compassion, Andrew's shame runs the show—unchecked and merciless. It is devastating his relationship with himself and his relationship with his wife. And, by the way, his shame-loaded story of who he is also compromises his ability to get a job, as it keeps him from proactively and confidently reaching out and advocating for himself. There is no doubt about it, Andrew is stuck, and in order to get out, he *must* get on his own team.

Shame: A Wily Competitor

As Andrew and Nicole's story shows, shame packs a "one-two punch," hurting not only our relationship with ourselves but also our relationship with the people we love. In spite of this, shame is a common emotion. We may wish to never feel shame, but it's more reasonable to expect that we *will* feel shame from time to time. Relational self-awareness then means knowing how to identify it and how to work with it when we feel it creeping up on us.

First things first: shame and guilt are different. If we have done something that hurts someone we care about, we will likely experience feelings of guilt, and these feelings can actually be helpful—a sort of red flag from within letting us know that we have wandered from who and how we want to be. Guilt can serve as a motivator. Our guilty feelings lead us to make a repair with the person we have hurt. Our guilty feelings may drive us to take a fearless look at ourselves and our choices. Guilt tends to be specific and fixable—it is about what we have done and how to repair it.

Shame is different. Shame is more diffuse and static. Shame is about who we *are*. Guilt says, "I did something wrong," and shame says, "I am wrong." And, unlike guilt, which may drive us to be more conscientious and thoughtful, shame is an ineffective and cruel motivator. Shame is sneaky. It offers the illusion of being a motivator, lulling us into thinking that we *need* it in order to do what needs to be done.

Andrew is sure that unless he continues to berate himself, he will stop trying to look for a job at all. Shame keeps him from seeing how, in fact, the opposite is possible and preferable—that he could motivate himself from a place of self-compassion. And unlike guilt, which can be used to drive us to repair a relational problem, shame compromises connection between self and other. This is the case with Andrew and Nicole. Andrew's shame creates painful distance and disengagement in his intimate relationship. This is true for all of us: *I can only love you to the degree that I love myself.*

Self-Compassion: I Am on My Own Team

Self-compassion is a powerful antidote to shame. In fact, it's really the only antidote to shame. The heart of self-compassion is deep friendship with one's self—I am on my own team. Self-compassion is not a new idea here, as it has shown up in various places throughout the book. Every time we engage in the Name-Connect-Choose process, we are practicing self-compassion, because we are attending to and valuing what lies within us. Every time we enact healthy boundaries by saying yes when we mean yes and no when we mean no, we are practicing self-compassion. Every time we return our attention to the present moment, dropping self-criticism and negative self-talk, we are practicing self-compassion.

So what is self-compassion? Dr. Kristin Neff (2011; 2012), the leading researcher in this area, says there are three elements of self-compassion:

- **Self-kindness.** "Self-compassion entails being warm and understanding toward ourselves when we suffer, fail, or feel inadequate, rather than ignoring our pain or flagellating ourselves with self-criticism."

- **Common humanity.** Being compassionate with ourselves involves recognizing that "suffering and personal inadequacy are part of the shared human experience." Shame says, "I am the only one who feels like this." Self-compassion says, "Everyone screws up or feels lousy from time to time."

- **Mindfulness.** When we are mindful, we bring our attention into the present moment (neither fast-forwarding to an imagined catastrophic future nor rewinding to old stories about the past), and we adopt a nonjudgmental and receptive state of mind in which we observe our thoughts and feelings rather than trying to suppress or deny them. Mindfulness is the difference between thinking, "I am such a loser" and thinking, "Oh, here comes that old, played-out story about how I am such a loser. I had better figure out how to be compassionate with myself in the face of this bull."

Self-compassion is not the same as self-esteem. It's not about hollowly propping yourself up or mindlessly offering yourself affirmations about your awesomeness. Self-compassion is also not about letting yourself off the hook. It is about embracing your imperfections and making a commitment to be gentle with yourself. As Dr. Neff says, self-compassion is about treating yourself the way you would treat a good friend. Life is hard and full of unforeseen challenges and disappointments—all of which are much easier to navigate when you are on your own team.

Self-Compassion in the Name of Love

My work with Andrew and Nicole continues, bit by bit and step by step. Andrew recently decided to begin individual therapy in order to address the roots of his shame. He told Nicole that he was only going to individual therapy "for her." Rather than feeling discouraged by his continued difficulty claiming that his well-being is worth fighting for, I shared with him that I think that's an act of relational heroism (Real 1998). Tackling his lack of self-compassion head-on is a way of fighting for his marriage. His marriage is so valuable to him that even though he would not be able to declare for himself that he is worth fighting for, he is willing to do it for love. It is my hope that, over time, he will take his emotional well-being seriously, but for right now, self-compassion in the name of love will have to be enough.

Even though we all deserve to be compassionate with ourselves for our own sake (because we are worthy of such gentleness), sometimes we need a different kind of motivation. We can motivate ourselves to practice self-compassion in order to be a more open-hearted intimate partner, parent, or friend. Whatever your motivation, see what happens when you commit to living and loving with self-compassion.

Steps Toward Loving Bravely

We must relate to ourselves with compassion in order to be able to offer the same to our intimate partner.

Comfort Meditation

The seeds of self-compassion are planted by those who have shown compassion to us, especially when we were young. This exercise is intended to help you identify who in your life has provided you with comfort—whose words and actions have helped you feel better. As Peggy O'Mara (former editor of *Mothering* magazine) says, "The way we talk to our children becomes their inner voice."

Begin by meditating on the idea of comfort. Sit quietly with your eyes closed, and bring forth images of comfort. Who in your life offers or has offered you comfort in a way that felt "just right"? Imagine you are on your back looking up at the sky. As a memory of comfort comes into your awareness, imagine it is a soft cloud moving into your line of vision. Sit with this memory for a few moments. What were you upset about? What did that person say or do that was so helpful? Why? As you connect with the memory, notice what you feel in your body and where you feel it. Then imagine the cloud moving away, out of your line of vision. Sit quietly and notice whether another memory of comfort comes up for you. If so, connect with it. When you are done with this meditation, write about the memory or memories that came up for you. Write about the people who offered you comfort and what they said or did.

Those Who Dwell Within

The next time you are having a hard time—feeling irritable, feeling weepy, or wanting to isolate yourself—turn your attention inward and notice how you are talking to yourself. Are you treating yourself harshly? Are you feeling shame? If so, what happens if you pull up one of the comfort memories you identified in the previous meditation? What happens if you begin to talk to yourself the way this person would talk to you? Does the shame begin to feel more like self-compassion? Do you find yourself beginning to feel more relaxed, open, and calm?

Care of the Self

Photocopy or download (from http://www.newharbinger.com/35814) the following list of common self-soothing strategies and keep it handy for times when you need it. Feel free to add your own!

- Talk to a friend, intimate partner, or family member.
- Write in your journal.
- Take a bath.
- Get out in nature.
- Do yoga or another form of exercise.
- Hang out with a pet.
- Watch TV or a movie.
- Sing.
- Dance.
- Paint, draw, or color.
- Cook.
- Build something.
- Clean.
- Meditate.

Lesson 20

Ride the Waves

To listen to your soul is to stop fighting with life—to stop fighting when things fall apart; when they don't go our way, when we get sick, when we are betrayed or mistreated or misunderstood.

—Elizabeth Lesser

During the last few days, I have been noticing my reactions to writing this final lesson. I watch myself sit down at my computer, fully intent on writing, but suddenly everything else takes precedence—an Instagram post, a phone call, a snack. This is a new and different problem for me, so I have been wondering what to make of it. I notice the fear-loaded questions that accompany my dillydallying—*Is this writer's block? What if it never lifts? What if I miss my deadline?*

I *name* these fear-loaded stories what they are, which allows me to dive a little deeper. As I quiet my mind and turn my attention inward to my emotional world, I *connect* to sadness rising up. I am sad to be finishing this book, as I deeply enjoy my quiet writing days, music in the background, dog in my lap. This chapter of my life is ending, and I don't feel quite ready to let it go.

This lesson, "Ride the Waves," is about trusting life—so it's fitting that this is exactly what I need to do in order to write it. This lesson is about how much more open we are to love when we allow rather than force, wonder instead of control, and exhale deeply into all that we do not know and cannot know. Although each lesson in this book certainly reflects some aspect of my own growing edges, no lesson captures my core challenge as a human being more than this lesson does. *Aha*, I think to myself. *No wonder my attention is everywhere but here.* I allow myself to sit with this awareness. I put one hand on my heart and take some deep breaths, sending some compassion to myself.

For so many of us, making that internal shift from *resisting* to *allowing* is really difficult, and we can get ourselves quite stuck fighting against reality as it exists right here and right now (bills, flat tires, and all). Dan Siegel describes it as the difference between a "no" space and a "yes" space (2010). When we're caught up in that "no" space, not only do we create suffering within ourselves, but our intimate relationship also pays a price. To our partner we are likely to feel prickly and hard to approach. Our partner may feel as if he or she is walking on eggshells. There's no doubt, intimate relationships go more smoothly when we commit ourselves to not letting the rigid and controlling parts of ourselves run the show. But that can feel easier said than done. What can help us make that all-important shift from *no* to *yes*? Our trusted Name-Connect-Choose process!

The first step is to *name* it ("There I go again, wanting answers that I cannot have yet, and struggling to sit in the unknown.") Next, we can *connect* with how this impatient and mistrustful place feels inside—the heaviness in the belly, the tightness in the chest, the swirling inside of the head. Inhale deeply and slowly and whisper, "Don't know" on the exhale. Finally, we can *choose* to redirect ourselves. We may choose to direct our attention toward someone we love, as turning toward a relational connection invites us to be present, giving us comfort or at least distraction. All we really can ever trust is the present moment anyway, so we may as well dive into it. Or we may choose to direct our attention to a task at hand, finding some little piece of the universe that we actually *can* control—a load of laundry, a piece of music, or an e-mail. Or we may choose to shift our energy with physical movement—a workout, shooting some baskets, or walking the dog. Or we may choose to rest.

I know that when I can shift myself into a space of greater surrender and trust, I can engage more deeply and happily in my intimate relationship, and this is true for all of us. The goal I have is to allow myself to ride waves of life and to trust myself as I do. That is a mighty goal for all of us. *The waves are within us and the waves are life itself.* Riding the waves that arise within means allowing ourselves to visit the full array of human emotions—from fear, to despair, to ecstasy—and return to a middle ground. Riding the waves of life is an invitation to meet life on life's terms—terms that may be quite different from what we had imagined, planned for, and aspired to. Elizabeth Lesser, who is quoted in the beginning of this lesson, offers a beautiful image for this moment: when we find ourselves paddling furiously against the current, it is time to let go of the oars. As she says, the secret is "to slow down, to feel deeply, to see ourselves clearly, to surrender to discomfort and uncertainty and to wait" (Lesser 2005, 270). Surrendering like this requires self-awareness, and it also grows self-awareness.

Thinking My Way Into Trust

Sometimes, as in my example above, we can give *ourselves* what we need to slow down and let go of angst, but sometimes we need a little help from a trustworthy guide. Our goal is to create an intimate relationship in which our partner can serve as that trustworthy guide when we need him or her to lead. And vice versa. It's all a big circle—riding the waves opens us to love more deeply in an intimate relationship, and an intimate relationship also helps us more effectively ride the waves.

Here's an example of how an intimate relationship can help us inhabit that "yes" space of sweet surrender. Our son, Brian, was about nine years old, and it was the day of his piano recital. He was nervous, and we were doing our best to help him manage his nerves. Everything seemed to be clicking along until the performance began, at which point he started to whisper to us that he couldn't do it. Todd and I took him out into the hallway and tried to help him feel better. Nothing was working, and he was getting increasingly upset.

Todd pulled me aside and said, "Al, it's not happening. We have to let it go." I could feel the full force of my resistance kick in. "Of course he's doing it. He has to do it. His name is in the program. The program has begun. There's no way to let his teacher know. He's got to rally." After another minute or so of discussion, it clicked for me, and I will never forget how it felt. Here's what I said to myself: *Todd feels clear. He has let this go. He is okay with letting this go. I trust Todd. I can let go.*

I had to *think* my way into surrender with logic, not emotion, as my guide. The grip of my resistance was tight, but each thought loosened me, finger by finger—*Todd feels clear. He has let this go. He is okay with letting this go. I trust Todd. I can let go.* I have every confidence that without Todd as my guide, I would have remained stuck in that moment with Brian, going round and round, fighting with the reality of the moment. I used my relationship with Todd to ride what was a truly mighty wave. Am I taking the imagery too far if I say that Todd was my surfboard?

So, we made our decision. Brian was not going to get onstage. The three of us walked back into the auditorium. I snuck onstage between performers and whispered in his teacher's ear. When I returned to our seats, Brian was sitting between his uncle and his older cousin. Both guys had their arms around him, and his uncle kissed the top of his head. I took my seat in the row behind Brian, and tears streamed down my face. When I let go of my old panicky story that we have to fight, push, and control in order for things to be okay, another definition of okay bloomed right in front of my eyes. Our son sat enveloped in the arms of men who love him. He was okay. The moment was okay. I watched him be granted the opportunity to know that the love he receives is not contingent on whether he is performing—literally!

My ability to surrender to Todd was good for our relationship. My leaning on Todd affirmed to *him* how much he means to me, and my willingness to lean on him affirmed to *me* that I don't have to do it all alone. I feel emotional as I write this, even though it happened years ago, because it captures for me the heart of an intimate relationship. We cannot do it on our own. None of us can. And in an intimate relationship, we don't have to. When we are caught up fighting with life, our partner may not be, so we can soften and lean on the relationship, trusting that's exactly what it is there for.

"How About That?!"

Some of us need a little help from a friend in order to find that state of surrender. Others of us live there every day, making surrender into a *trait*, not just a *state*. My friend Annie Burnside is a writer who hosts "soul circles" in her home—a spiritual book club of sorts. At one gathering, she shared a story that stuck with me and that shows how riding the waves can really be a way of life. The story is of a couple who attribute their happiness in life and in love to their motto: "How about that?!" This is a motto they use whenever the "stuff" hits the fan...when life happens. Their basement floods. "How about that?!" They get lost on the way to an appointment. "How about that?!" Someone gets sick. "How about that?!" (Burnside 2014).

Now, I am sure these lovebirds get cranky and irritable at times, but they have committed themselves to moving with, rather than against, the flow of life. Their willingness to anchor themselves with this motto is good for each of them individually—it's a great stress reducer. And it's good for them as a couple. It reduces blame and defensiveness ("We don't have to figure out who made us get lost") while increasing a sense of teamwork ("What are *we* going to do about this flooded basement?").

Love Is Alive

Love is alive. Love is ever-changing. Love ebbs and flows. In a recent therapy session, an unhappy wife said to her husband, "We aren't the same as we used to be. Why can't it be like it was when we were first married?" Her tone was critical, and her attitude was passive. It's hard to imagine our "How about that?!" couple saying the same, isn't it? They might say, "We aren't the same as we used to be. How about that?!" and go on to explore together how love changes and how those changes must be met with gentle curiosity and a healthy dose of humor. How unfair it is to expect an intimate relationship, an unfolding love story, to stay the way it was. Love changes over time—day to day, month to month, and year to year. Holding love to a standard that reflects the past or the future is surely a recipe for disappointment.

Staying open to life's unfolding in general and love's unfolding in particular requires that we trust ourselves, that we rely on our resilience, and that we stand up again when we fall down. Several years ago a student of mine introduced me to a metaphor that really captures our journey with love. The metaphor is of *kintsugi*, which is a Japanese ceramics technique. In kintsugi, the artist takes a broken ceramic object and reassembles it, holding the pieces together with resin mixed with gold, silver, or platinum. The cracks are not to be hidden but instead made beautiful. Like ceramics restored through kintsugi, each of us can experience priceless growth from disappointment and heartbreak, and isn't that what riding the waves is all about? Love will never be easy or pain-free, but we can trust that there is strength and beauty—even in and *especially* in—all the broken places.

Steps Toward Loving Bravely

Fighting against change—holding tight to our expectations as life unfolds in a different direction—keeps us from loving bravely and deeply.

The Serenity Prayer

It is likely that you have come across the Serenity Prayer at some point in your life, but have you meditated on it? When we are willing to embody the words of the Serenity Prayer, commonly attributed to

Reinhold Niebuhr and adapted by AA, we open ourselves up for connection by agreeing to meet life on life's terms. Aspiring to know when to advocate for change and when to let go is vital in an intimate relationship. We will never do it perfectly, and that is not the goal. Here are the words:

Grant me the serenity to accept the things I cannot change,
The courage to change the things I can,
And the wisdom to know the difference.

Sit quietly, reflect on these words, and notice what comes up for you.

- In which areas of your life are you most wise—able to discern the changeable from the unchangeable?

- In which areas of your life is it especially difficult to know when to push and when to let go?

- Are there certain relationships in which you are better able to embody the Serenity Prayer and others in which it is harder for you?

Takeaways

You did it! You have reached the last exercise of the last lesson of this book. Congratulations. It's quite an accomplishment. This book is a deep dive with no easy answers and no shortcuts. These exercises have given you an opportunity to grow your relational self-awareness. It is likely that you have connected dots in ways you had not done before, had conversations you had not had before, and experimented with practices that are new to your life.

To consolidate your learning, look back over the journal entries you've written and highlight what really stood out for you. Write yourself a top-ten list of "aha moments"—insights, connections, or learnings—that you are taking away from this journey into yourself. Post your "ahas" somewhere so you can make reference to them.

Conclusion

Before I began writing this book, I knew exactly how I wanted to end it—with my favorite poem. I read this poem each year on the last day of class, and I read it at my brother and sister-in-law's wedding. Written by Oriah Mountain Dreamer (1995), "The Invitation" captures the very essence of an intimate relationship. This poem is a reminder that love is far from neat and tidy; love is an invitation to brave and messy authenticity. In order to respond to the sacred invitation to love and be loved, we must first extend that invitation to ourselves. We must know, understand, and love ourselves with such devotion and ferocity that the love of another serves as an extension, a mirror, and a validation of that love. That is the love that I wish for you, my dear reader.

The Invitation
It doesn't interest me
what you do for a living.
I want to know
what you ache for
and if you dare to dream
of meeting your heart's longing.

It doesn't interest me
how old you are.
I want to know
if you will risk
looking like a fool
for love
for your dream
for the adventure of being alive.

It doesn't interest me
what planets are
squaring your moon...
I want to know
if you have touched
the centre of your own sorrow
if you have been opened
by life's betrayals
or have become shriveled and closed
from fear of further pain.

I want to know
if you can sit with pain
mine or your own
without moving to hide it
or fade it
or fix it.

I want to know
if you can be with joy
mine or your own
if you can dance with wildness
and let the ecstasy fill you
to the tips of your fingers and toes
without cautioning us
to be careful
to be realistic
to remember the limitations
of being human.

It doesn't interest me
if the story you are telling me
is true.
I want to know if you can
disappoint another
to be true to yourself.
If you can bear
the accusation of betrayal
and not betray your own soul.
If you can be faithless
and therefore trustworthy.

I want to know if you can see Beauty
even when it is not pretty
every day.
And if you can source your own life
from its presence.

I want to know
if you can live with failure
yours and mine
and still stand at the edge of the lake
and shout to the silver of the full moon,
"Yes."

It doesn't interest me
to know where you live
or how much money you have.
I want to know if you can get up
after the night of grief and despair
weary and bruised to the bone
and do what needs to be done
to feed the children.

It doesn't interest me
who you know
or how you came to be here.
I want to know if you will stand
in the centre of the fire
with me
and not shrink back.

It doesn't interest me
where or what or with whom
you have studied.
I want to know
what sustains you
from the inside
when all else falls away.

I want to know
if you can be alone
with yourself
and if you truly like
the company you keep
in the empty moments.

Acknowledgments

I am truly grateful to have had the opportunity to write this book. This book is about the sacred and precious nature of relationships, and I am aware that without my *tribe*, this book would *never* have happened.

I want to acknowledge my agent, Jill Marsal, at Marsal Lyon Literary Agency, who responds to e-mails usually before I have hit send and whose advice is sage and kind. Thank you to my publicist, Dana Kaye, at Kaye Publicity, for all of your hard work and optimism. My editors Melissa Kirk, Melissa Valentine, Clancy Drake, Marisa Solís, and Erin Raber challenged me to grow as a writer while remaining enthusiastic. Thank you also to the whole team at New Harbinger Publications. Leslie Basa, Stephanie Gray, Neil Venketramen, and Dan Rosenberg, thank you for your wisdom and guidance. Bonnie Lessing, you are a steady and graceful presence in my world. Thank you, Jamilli Alpuche, for everything you do to keep our family afloat.

I never would have completed this project without my amazing team of graduate assistants: Monique Brown, Danielle Carlson, Tom Kennedy, and Rachel Zar. Monique, you have been a champion of this project since day one. Rachel, you are a gifted editor. Danielle, you ask brilliant questions that push my thinking. Tom, your thoughtfulness and work ethic have been invaluable. The four of you kept me on track and inspired for many months. I have loved sharing every step of this process with you.

I am blessed with the most amazing friends anybody could ask for—friends who accept me as I am while challenging me to grow. Zulus (Ali, Julee, and Lynn), we have been studying love in our very own four-girl love lab since we were in elementary school, sharing with each other first crushes, first kisses, heartbreaks, wedding days, births, and every moment in between. What I have learned from *us* is on every page of this book. Ali, you are truly my soul sister—in writing and in life. Julee, you ground me and inspire me—"The book is real." Lynnie, you believe in me even when I do not. I am also blessed with the support of my 'hood girls, my swole sister, Lisa, and #Glennfit. Finally, my sweet Soul Circle (Kim, Eve, Karen, Kathy, Julie, Julia, Becca, and Rebecca), you honored my "empowered woman" and comforted my "little girl" every step of the way.

Thank you, Mona Fishbane, for being endlessly generous with your wisdom and your love, and thank you for the gift of your foreword. I want to acknowledge my home away from home, the Family Institute at Northwestern University, for providing me with my intellectual foundation and for supporting my ambition. Thank you, Jana Jones, Cheryl Rampage, Doug Breunlin, Nancy Burgoyne, and Anthony Chambers, for your encouragement. Thank you, Bill Pinsof and Art Nielsen, for giving life to the "Marriage 101" course that I love so dearly. I am endlessly grateful to my students, graduate and undergraduate, who bring their full selves to my classroom and allow me to bring mine. Your questions, challenges, stories, and journeys inspire me. Thank you to my therapy clients who invite me into their innermost rooms and show me what loving bravely is all about.

The love lessons I learned from the family I grew up in are in the pages of this book, so I want to thank them for being with me on this journey: Christine, Fred John, Gerry Jr., Matt, Johanna, Addison, Connor, Ian, Reese, Gretchen, Maddie, and Molly. My mother's love of books and her infinite belief in me certainly inspired me to dare greatly, and the sweet spirit of my father, Gerry, has been a comfort to me during this process. When I made the best decision of my life, marrying Todd Solomon, I inherited his amazing family, whom I love dearly: Ellen, Ken, David, Tanya, Matt, Mollie, Michael, Bonni, Mimi, and Jake. Thank you for always making me laugh, Team Solomon.

And, most important, I want to thank my family. Todd, you are my rock and my true north. I would never have had the courage to tackle this book without your support and your love. I am blessed beyond measure. This book never would have happened without your willingness to give me long stretches of uninterrupted writing time by taking our children overnight to a whole host of random local suburban hotels. Our marriage is my home. Brian and Courtney, when I told you I was going to write a book, the first thing each of you asked (in separate conversations) was, "Will it mean we have less time with you?" Your love for me means everything. I am so grateful for the interest you have shown—your offers to edit, draw the cover, even publish it show what caring souls you are. I am grateful for your patience and forgiveness for all the ways, big and small, that this book has been part of our family. Thank you to the littlest member of our family, Sawyer the schnoodle, who has been my faithful and sleepy writing companion.

Appendix 1

Trauma

This appendix is for readers who need to weave one or more traumatic chapters into the story of their lives in order to move forward and love bravely.

Psychological trauma is an emotional response to a terrible event. There are two main types of traumatic events: one-time traumas and enduring traumas. *One-time traumas* include surviving a terrible incident, like a crime (being sexually assaulted, robbed, or otherwise attacked) or a natural disaster (tornado, hurricane, or flood). *Enduring traumas* involve an ongoing relationship and include surviving emotional, physical, or sexual abuse; domestic violence; neglect; kidnapping; bullying; or even growing up in a family dealing with addiction. Traumatic events are those in which someone is exposed to actual or threatened death, serious injury, or sexual violation. Traumatic events can leave a variety of scars. Initially following the event, people may suffer from shock or denial. Over the long term, people may experience unpredictable emotions, flashbacks, relationship problems, and even physical symptoms like headaches and nausea. These are signs of post-traumatic stress disorder (PTSD).

When traumas endure over many months or years—as is the case with growing up in an abusive home or being in an abusive intimate relationship—they can result in relationship problems, physical problems, difficulty regulating emotions, dissociation or losing time, struggles with impulse control, cognitive issues (such as attention problems or executive functioning problems), and lack of self-esteem or poor self-concept. Therapists sometimes refer to symptoms such as these as *complex trauma*.

People who suffer trauma early in their lives (as kids or teens) are particularly at risk of pushing away memories and feelings about the trauma, determined that nobody has to know and believing that it will not affect who they are. While I respect the desire not to be defined by trauma, what I see over and over is that, even if you *think* that your traumatic memories are stuffed away, something happens to make them sneak out sooner or later. *Often that something is falling in love!*

An intimate relationship requires you to become vulnerable to another person, sharing stories of the past and hopes for the future. In that sharing, you may begin to feel that you want your partner to know about your trauma. Or, as your partner gets to know more and more about you, it may feel like a glaring omission for her not to know something so significant about you. But that urge to open up might be coupled with a fear that if your partner were to know this about you, she couldn't possibly still love you.

Knowing when and how to share traumatic chapters of your story rests upon healthy *boundary management*. One extreme is having *diffuse boundaries*, which means you may tell someone everything about you as soon as you start dating. Sometimes people rationalize this approach by thinking, "I'd rather know now if you can't handle all of me, so that I don't invest needless time and emotion." The other extreme is *rigid boundaries*, which means you may wait and wait, perhaps hoping the other person will never find out. Sometimes people who take this route think, "If you were to know this about me, you couldn't love me." The desire to keep the past stuffed in the far recesses of our minds is usually motivated by shame, but doing so also perpetuates shame. *Healthy boundaries*—being both connected and protected—lie in the shades of gray between these extremes. Sharing your story requires people, and sharing your stories builds trust between people. Trust is essential in a healthy intimate relationship.

Trust and trauma unfortunately go hand in hand. Trauma (especially complex trauma) involves a breach of trust in an important relationship (for example, in the case of sexual abuse). Therefore, building an intimate, trusting romantic relationship is, by its very nature, *re-traumatizing*, as the intimate relationship ends up in some ways replicating the old traumatic relationship. For example, some people notice that in the context of their intimate relationship, sometimes especially during sex, they experience an increase in flashbacks or intrusive thoughts (uninvited thoughts that pop into your head) related to the trauma. If this happens, the best course of action is to do some individual psychotherapy with a therapist who specializes in trauma. Appendix 2 has information about how to find a therapist.

A loving, trusting romantic relationship can be a powerfully healing force in the life of someone who has suffered a trauma. This is the best-case scenario, and it is possible. I have been moved to tears many times in therapy when an intimate partner takes the risk of bravely sharing a painful memory from his or her past. In those moments, courage claims victory over shame. And there is no more powerful way to heal shame than through the power of connection. But self-work and self-care in the form of taking responsibility for the impact that the trauma has had on you lay the foundation. In other words, your romantic partner cannot heal your trauma. Love alone is not enough.

Appendix 2

How to Find a Therapist

It is brave, indeed, to decide that it's time to start going to therapy! Because it is emotionally taxing enough to decide it's time to ask for help, you at least want the task of finding a therapist to be an easy one. This appendix is intended to make your search as seamless as possible.

Finding a Therapist

There is more than one way to get to a first session. Here are some options for getting a referral:

- Ask your primary care physician for a few names.

- Talk to a friend or family member who is in therapy and find out whether that therapist will also see you or refer you to a colleague.

- Call your health insurance carrier and ask for a list of providers in your area. You can then look on providers' websites or call them to learn about the services they offer.

- Search online using one of the websites listed below.

Choosing a Therapist

Creating a relationship with a therapist is a big deal, and in order to benefit from this trusting relationship, you will need to be vulnerable, honest, and accountable. Therefore, be discerning and careful in choosing someone with whom you can work. I suggest that you do the following:

- **Identify a few possible candidates and then talk to each of them on the phone or do a first session.** You and the therapist will *both* need to assess how the relationship feels. Even if a therapist is competent, there might not be great chemistry between the two of you, so it is okay to do more than one first session. Not unlike an intimate relationship, the way you feel about your therapist at session one will be different than the way you will feel at session ten, but you still will need to access your gut feelings during the first session: How safe do you feel? How listened to do you feel? How trusting do you feel?

- **Remember, you are the consumer.** It is appropriate to ask specific questions on the phone and in your initial session. Questions you might want to ask your therapist include:
  - Can you tell me about your training?
  - How would you describe your approach to therapy?
  - Can you tell me about your experience working with clients like me?
  - How will we create treatment goals, and how will we monitor my progress?
  - Do you feel you can help me?

- **Talk with your therapist about the reactions that you are having to your sessions.** If you feel misunderstood or rushed, say so. If you have a question about how your therapist is viewing you or your situation, ask. Talking with your therapist about the relationship *between the two of you* will help you in your other relationships—including in your intimate relationship—so speak up!

- **If you are hiring a couples therapist, ask about his or her training.** Being a good therapist and being a good couples therapist are quite different, so either seek therapy from someone whose name is followed by the letters LMFT (licensed marriage and family therapist) or ensure that that clinician has extensive training in working with couples. The online resource list that follows includes some websites specifically for those seeking couples therapy.

Online Resources

Here are some online resources that you can use on your quest to find a therapist.

General Websites

- *Psychology Today*: http://www.psychologytoday.com

- Good Therapy: http://www.goodtherapy.org

- Network Therapy: http://www.networktherapy.com

- All Therapist: http://www.alltherapist.com

- All About Counseling: http://www.allaboutconseling.com

Couples and Family Therapy

- American Association for Marriage and Family Therapy: http://www.aamft.org

- Center for Self Leadership: http://www.selfleadership.org

- The International Centre for Excellence in Emotionally Focused Therapy: http://www.iceeft.com

- Imago Relationships: http://www.gettingtheloveyouwant.com

Sex Therapy

- Society for Sex Therapy and Research: http://sstarnet.org /therapist-directory.php

- American Association of Sexuality Educators, Counselors and Therapists: http://www.aasect.org/referral-directory

References

Ansari, A. 2015. *Modern Romance*. With E. Klinenberg. New York: Penguin Press.

Bosman, J. 2014. "For *Fifty Shades of Grey*, More than 100 Million Sold." *The New York Times*. Accessed April 2016. http://www.nytimes.com/2014/02/27/business/media/for-fifty-shades-of-grey-more-than-100-million-sold.html?_r=1.

Brown, B. 2015. *Daring Greatly: How the Courage to Be Vulnerable Transforms the Way We Live, Love, Parent, and Lead*. New York: Avery.

Burnside, A. 2014. *From Role to Soul: 15 Shifts on the Awakening Journey*. Deadwood, OR: Wyatt-MacKenzie Publishing.

Chapman, G. 2015. *The 5 Love Languages: The Secret to Love that Lasts*. Chicago: Northfield Publishing.

Coontz, S. 2006. *Marriage, a History: How Love Conquered Marriage*. New York: Penguin.

Doherty, W. 2013. *Take Back Your Marriage: Sticking Together in a World That Pulls Us Apart* (Second Edition). New York: Guilford Press.

Finkel, E. 2013. "The Hack to Save Your Marriage." TEDxUChicago.

Finkel, E. J., E. B. Slotter, L. B. Luchies, G. M. Walton, and J. J. Gross. 2013. "A Brief Intervention to Promote Conflict Reappraisal Preserves Marital Quality over Time." *Psychological Science* 24(8): 1595–1601.

Fishbane, M. 2013. *Loving with the Brain in Mind: Neurobiology and Couple Therapy*. New York: W.W. Norton & Company, Inc.

Fisher, H. 2004. *Why We Love: The Nature and Chemistry of Romantic Love*. New York: Henry Holt.

Freitas, D. 2013. *The End of Sex: How Hookup Culture Is Leaving a Generation Unhappy, Sexually Unfulfilled, and Confused about Intimacy*. New York: Basic Books.

Gilbert, E. 2007. *Eat, Pray, Love: One Woman's Search for Everything Across Italy, India, and Indonesia*. New York: Riverhead Books.

Gordon, C. L., R. A. M. Arnette, and R. E. Smith. 2011. "Have You Thanked Your Spouse Today?: Felt and Expressed Gratitude Among Married Couples." *Personality and Individual Differences* 50: 339–343.

Gottman, J. M. 2011. *The Science of Trust: Emotional Attunement for Couples.* New York: W.W. Norton & Company.

hooks, b. 2001. *All About Love: New Visions.* New York: William Morrow Paperbacks.

Johns, K. N., E. S. Allen, and K. C. Gordon. 2015. "The Relationship Between Mindfulness and Forgiveness in Infidelity." *Mindfulness* 6: 1462–1471.

Johnson, S. 2008. *Hold Me Tight: Seven Conversations for a Lifetime of Love.* New York: Little, Brown and Company.

Johnson, S. 2013. *Love Sense: The Revolutionary New Science of Romantic Relationships.* New York: Little, Brown and Company.

Kornfield, J. 2016. "Forgiveness Meditation." Accessed April 2016. https://jackkornfield.com/forgiveness-meditation.

Krasnow, I. 2011. *The Secret Lives of Wives: Women Share What It Really Takes to Stay Married.* New York: Gotham.

———. 2016. "Seven Secrets to Staying Married." Accessed April 2016. http://iriskrasnow.com/_secret_lives/seven_secrets.htm.

Lawler-Row, K. A., J. C. Karremans, C. Scott, M. Edlis-Matityahou, and L. Edwards. 2008. "Forgiveness, Physiological Reactivity and Health: The Role of Anger." *International Journal of Psychophysiology* 68: 51–58.

Lee, S. W. S., and N. Schwartz. 2014. "Framing Love: When It Hurts to Think We Were Made for Each Other." *Journal of Experimental Social Psychology* 54: 61–67.

Lesser, E. 2000. *The Seeker's Guide.* New York: Villard.

———. 2005. *Broken Open.* New York: Villard.

Lewicki, R. J., B. Polin, and R. B. Lount Jr. 2016. "An Exploration of the Structure of Effective Apologies." *Negotiation and Conflict Management Research* 9(2): 177–196.

Linehan, M. M. 2015. *DBT Skills Training Manual: Second Edition.* New York: Guilford Press.

Lyubomirsky, S. 2013. *The Myths of Happiness: What Should Make You Happy but Doesn't, What Shouldn't Make You Happy but Does.* London: Penguin Books.

Malec, A. B. 2015. *Marriage in Modern Life: Why It Works When It Works.* Charleston, SC: Advantage Media Group.

Markman, H. J., and S. M. Stanley. 2010. *Fighting for Your Marriage: A Deluxe Revised Edition of the Classic Best-seller for Enhancing Your Marriage and Preventing Divorce.* San Francisco: Jossey-Bass.

McAdams, D. 2006. "The Role of Narrative in Personality Psychology Today." *Narrative Inquiry* 16(1): 11–18.

Moore, T. 1996. *Soul Mates: Honoring the Mystery of Love and Relationship.* New York: Harper Perennial.

Myss, C. 1997. *Why People Don't Heal and How They Can.* New York: Harmony.

Neff, K. D. 2012. "The Science of Self-Compassion." In *Compassion and Wisdom:* 79–92, edited by Alan S. Gurman and R. Siegel. New York: Guilford Press.

Neff, K. 2011. *Self-Compassion: The Proven Power of Being Kind to Yourself.* New York: HarperCollins.

Nhat Hanh, Thich. 2011. *Fidelity: How to Create a Loving Relationship That Lasts.* Berkeley, CA: Parallax Press.

Oriah. 1999. *The Invitation.* San Francisco: HarperONE.

Parker-Pope, T. 2007. "Is It Love or Mental Illness? They're Closer Than You Think." *Wall Street Journal*, February 13.

Perel, E. 2007. *Mating in Captivity: Unlocking Erotic Intelligence.* New York: Harper Perennial.

Perel, E. 2015. "Why Happy Couples Cheat." TED Talk.

Pew Research Center. 2010. *The Decline of Marriage and the Rise of New Families.* Washington, D.C.: Pew Research Center, Social and Demographic Trends. http://www.pewsocialtrends.org/files/2010/11/pew-social-trends-2010-families.pdf.

Pinsof, W. M. 1995. *Integrative Problem-Centered Therapy: A Synthesis of Family, Individual, and Biological Therapies.* New York: Basic Books.

Pinsof, W. M., D. C. Breunlin, A. L. Chambers, A. H. Solomon, and W. P. Russell. 2015. "Integrative Problem-Centered Metaframeworks Approach." In *Clinical Handbook of Couple Therapy: Fifth Edition*, edited by Alan S. Gurman, Jay L. Lebow, and Douglas K. Snyder. New York: Guilford Press.

Przybylski, A. K., and N. Weinstein. 2012. "Can You Connect with Me Now? How the Presence of Mobile Communication Technology

Influences Face-to-Face Conversation Quality." *Journal of Social and Personal Relationships* 30(3): 237–246.

Real, T. 1998. *I Don't Want to Talk About It: Overcoming the Secret Legacy of Male Depression.* New York: Scribner.

Rock, D., and D. Siegel. 2011. "The Healthy Mind Platter." Accessed April 2016. http://healthymindplatter.com.

Schwartz, B. 2004. *The Paradox of Choice: Why More Is Less.* New York: HarperCollins.

Sheinkman, M., and M. Fishbane. 2004. "The Vulnerability Cycle: Working with Impasses in Couple Therapy." *Family Process* 43(3): 279–299.

Siegel, D. J. 2010. *Mindsight: The New Science of Personal Transformation.* New York: Bantam Books.

Siegel, D. J., and M. Hartzel. 2013. *Parenting from the Inside Out 10th-Anniversary Edition: How a Deeper Self-Understanding Can Help You Raise Children Who Thrive.* New York: TarcherPerigee.

Sollee, D. 2016. "Marriage Quotes." Accessed April 2016. http://www.smartmarriages.com/marriage.quotes.html.

Solomon, A. 2016. "Inside Hookup Culture: Are We Having Fun Yet?" *Psychotherapy Networker* January–February.

Solomon, A. H. 2001. *Stories of Us: A Qualitative Analysis of Sex Differences in the Relationship Narratives of Recently Married Women and Men.* Unpublished doctoral dissertation, Northwestern University, Evanston, IL.

Turkle, S. 2015. *Reclaiming Conversation: The Power of Talk in a Digital Age.* New York: Penguin Publishing Group.

Whisman, M., A. E. Dixon, and B. Johnson. 1997. "Therapists' Perspectives of Couple Problems and Treatment Issues in Couple Therapy." *Journal of Family Psychology* 11: 361–366.

Wilder, T. 1942. *The Skin of Our Teeth.* New York: Harper & Brothers.

Wile, D. 2002. "Collaborative Couple Therapy." In *Clinical Handbook of Couple Therapy: Third Edition,* edited by Alan S. Gurman and Neil S. Jacobson. New York: Guilford Press.

Wood, A. M., J. J. Froh, and A. W. A. Geraghty. 2010. "Gratitude and Well-Being: A Review and Theoretical Integration." *Clinical Psychology Review* 30: 890–905.

Alexandra H. Solomon, PhD, is staff clinical psychologist, member of the teaching faculty in the marriage and family therapy graduate program, and clinical assistant professor of psychology at The Family Institute at Northwestern University. In addition to her clinical work with couples and individuals, Solomon teaches graduate and undergraduate students. One of her courses is Northwestern University's internationally renowned "Building Loving and Lasting Relationships: Marriage 101," which combines traditional and experiential learning to educate students about key relational issues like intimacy, sex, conflict, acceptance, and forgiveness. Solomon's work has been widely cited, and her articles on love and marriage have appeared in *The Handbook of Clinical Psychology*, *The Handbook of Couple Therapy*, *Family Process*, *Psychotherapy Networker*, and other top publications in psychology. Her work also appears in *O Magazine* and *The Huffington Post*, and she is a frequent interviewee and contributor for the *Oprah Winfrey Network*, *Yahoo! Health*, *The Atlantic*, CBS *Early Show*, NPR, *Psychology Today*, and WGN *Morning News*. She is a sought-after speaker for corporate, collegiate, and professional audiences on topics related to modern love. Solomon lives in Highland Park, IL, with her husband, Todd, and their two children, Brian and Courtney.

Sign up for monthly articles and relationship advice from Alexandra at www.bit.do/lovingbravely, and learn more about her work at www .dralexandrasolomon.com.

Foreword writer, **Mona D. Fishbane, PhD**, is director of couple therapy training at the Chicago Center for Family Health, and a clinical psychologist in private practice. She is an AAMFT-approved supervisor, a member of the advisory board for the journal *Family Process*, and a long-term AFTA member, where she has served on the board. Fishbane lectures nationally and internationally, and has published numerous articles on couples therapy and neurobiology, as well as on intergenerational relationships. She has been the recipient of honors and fellowships, most recently a grant from the John Templeton Foundation. Fishbane's book, *Loving with the Brain in Mind*, is part of the Norton Series on interpersonal neurobiology. Find out more at www.mona fishbane.com.

MORE BOOKS *from*
NEW HARBINGER PUBLICATIONS

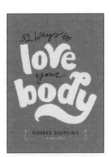
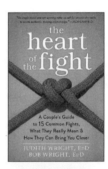

Register your **new harbinger** titles for additional benefits!

When you register your **new harbinger** title—purchased in any format, from any source—you get access to benefits like the following:

- Downloadable accessories like printable worksheets and extra content

- Instructional videos and audio files

- Information about updates, corrections, and new editions

Not every title has accessories, but we're adding new material all the time.

Access free accessories in 3 easy steps:

1. Sign in at NewHarbinger.com (or **register** to create an account).

2. Click on **register a book**. Search for your title and click the **register** button when it appears.

3. Click on the **book cover or title** to go to its details page. Click on **accessories** to view and access files.

That's all there is to it!

If you need help, visit:

NewHarbinger.com/accessories

new harbinger
CELEBRATING
40 YEARS